I0049368

FUN AT WORK

Greg Winteregg

Fun at Work
Greg Winteregg
©2019 Greg Winteregg. All rights reserved worldwide.

ISBN: 978-1-7336227-2-1 paperback
978-1-7336227-1-4 eBook

The author and publisher expressly disclaim all and any liability to any person, whether a purchaser of this publication or not, in respect of anything and of the consequences of anything done or omitted to be done by any such person in reliance, whether whole or partial, upon the whole or any part of the contents of publication.

This publication is intended to give the reader business information based on the author's personal experience. It is not advice and nothing in this publication should be considered legal or financial advice. The author is not a legal or financial advisor and no information is intended or may be construed as advice. Although the author uses his best endeavors to explain all relevant matters and instructions to you clearly, the reader may, however, misinterpret such explanations and/or instructions or may omit to read all instructions. The author is not liable in any respect for any such misinterpretations or omissions. The reader has either received his or her own independent professional advice or has made his or her own deliberate decision not to obtain the relevant advice and accepts any risks of having done so.

Cover Design: Claire Coziahr

MATTERHORN
BUSINESS DEVELOPMENT
IF YOU KNOW US, YOU WIN.

www.matterhornpress.com
(727) 810-3022

Dedication

At the risk of sounding cliché, I want to dedicate this book to anyone who has ever taken the risk of starting their own business. It takes courage, dedication, and persistence. It's never easy. It's not always successful.

This book is for you. I intend for it to help your current endeavor, or one that you are planning for the future. If you have been thrown from the horse, get back on and try again by using what I am teaching here from my experiences.

For me, there's no better feeling in the world than helping others with something that you have created. Here's to your success. Go forward. Flourish and Prosper.

Table of Contents

Author's Preface

I wrote this book to help everyone have more fun at work. That may sound strange to some. Is work really supposed to be 'fun'? Isn't it supposed to be a grind? After all, that is how we got, "Manic Monday" and how Wednesday became, "hump day." We get over the hump on our trip to, "TGIF" (Thank God It's Friday).

From these gems alone, we could conclude that many people think there is no place for fun in the work place.

Yet, I've always been able to make everything I've done a game. Even when my summer jobs included working in a factory making house trailers, cleaning up used cars to be re-sold, or helping on a construction site building a new home.

But I've had a few jobs that were no fun. I noticed that it totally affected my life and attitude if I worked in a job I didn't like.

Early Start

I was raised in the restaurant business. I learned about hard work at an early age; but I also learned about the freedom and choices owning your own business allows compared to working for someone else. Somewhere in my teens, I decided that I would always want to work for myself.

I also learned that there are good bosses and bad bosses, very good bosses and managers, and very bad bosses and managers. They had a lot to do with whether or not I enjoyed my job.

How about you? We surveyed hundreds of owners and managers while researching this book. You told us you want more time, money, control, and freedom. You also want to work with less stress and worry. I wrote each chapter with those objectives in mind. It is my intention to help you create your ideal life, at work and at home. I'm going to help you apply these principles to better any situation you may have.

You really can have Fun at Work.

Full Disclosure

I'm a dentist. I worked hard for my D.D.S.*—eight years of college. I debated putting Dr. in front of my name on the cover of the book, but I decided not to because dentists are notoriously bad business owners. Who wants to take business advice from a dentist?

Here's the short story of how I arrived at this day:

I graduated from dental school in 1981. After graduation, many of my classmates were going into military service, a residency or an associateship. Not me. I went into private practice. I had my practice purchase deal signed during the Thanksgiving break of my senior year of dental school— about eight months before I would be licensed to practice. That's how dedicated I was to owning my own business.

*D.D.S: Doctor of Dental Surgery

Fast forward eleven years: I was having no fun. Revenue was down. I had a hard time paying bills. I considered laying off staff. I had a hard time sleeping. I even thought about working for another dentist.

No fun.

Yet, I'd had about $60,000 dollars in practice management consulting from six different companies. None of it worked. To say I was stressed out was an understatement.

In 1992, I became a client at another practice management company. I learned about marketing, selling and managing and I aggressively applied what I learned. Twelve months later, I doubled the business, brought on an associate and office manager, and worked twenty-two hours a week instead of forty or more. I was basically semi-retired at age thirty-eight, and I was looking around the county for a second location.

That was the magic of learning real business basics and applying them to my practice. During that year, I figured out how my dad and uncle had been able to make a family restaurant in an Indiana farm town with three thousand people successful enough to put me, my brother, and my cousins through college.

Business basics are business basics.

In 1993, the management company offered me a partnership. I sold my practice and home to help more dentists end their struggle in the business of dentistry.

I succeeded in achieving that objective. Today that business is arguably the largest dental practice management training company in North America with clients in forty-eight states and five Canadian provinces.

I could write a book about all the bad/awful/potentially disastrous situations we've helped dentists avoid. We saved marriages for many. Prevented bankruptcy for others. I have letters and cards from some who were even considering suicide prior to getting basic business help. It doesn't get more satisfying than that.

I have doctors who have gone from struggling in business to owning multiple locations. One went from working for someone else to owning nine offices doing over ten million dollars a year. Another went from a million dollars in annual revenue to over thirty million. One showed up six months behind on rent and paid it all off in the first month of being trained on a few business basics.

It's common to go from working forty to sixty hours a week to getting an associate and working half of those hours, if any at all, while still owning the business. It's not hard, and it's a whole lot of fun.

After twenty-five years, I once again found myself semi-retired. I continued working part-time at the practice management company. But I threw myself into philanthropy* and helping non-profits. Then I started another company to teach management to non-dentists.

*philanthropy: goodwill to fellow members of the human race especially: active effort to promote human welfare

Business basics are business basics.

These business owners and managers are now achieving the same levels of success as the thousands of dentists I've helped.

I have over fifty years of experience in business. I have contributed to the lives of millions, maybe tens of millions, if you count all their patients and customers.

I have an ideal life. I've been married to the love of my life since 1980. I have three awesome kids that have either started their own businesses or assist me in mine. I help a lot of people. I control the things that I can control. I figure out how to take the things I can't control and turn them to my advantage as much as possible; all while being ethical, honest and remaining true to my goals and beliefs.

I have a basic rule:

If it's not fun, I'm not doing it.

I have fun with everything I do. That doesn't mean that I don't work late into the night or sometimes spend time away from my family. But I have a purpose to help others and that gives me incredible joy. I "work" hard at it.

This book was written to help you learn from my successes in business and life, as well as some of my mistakes. It doesn't matter if you own a business, manage one, or have aspirations to do so. There is something in here for everyone. You really can have "Fun At Work."

I want that for you. Not someone else's definition of it, but your very own. There are exercises for you to do as you go through the book to apply these principles of success. I will be here to offer as much help as you need.

No matter what your current circumstances, you can create your ideal life. Want more time, money, freedom or control with less stress and worry? Read on.

If you would like help in applying the concepts that I am writing about, you can get a free PDF of exercises I have created to help you get more out of reading "FUN AT WORK."

Simply go to www.funatworkthebook.com for the download.

If it's not fun, I'm not doing it.

Introduction

Let's talk about the great American dream. Work hard all your life, be frugal and save your money, pay off your house and cars, get out of debt, invest wisely, retire at age sixty-five, play golf, fish, relax, travel and enjoy life. It's all perfect. Just like Disney World.

But then real life isn't fantasy land. We get world wars, recessions, depressions, bubbles*, oil embargos, stock market crashes and terrorism. Not to mention layoffs, pay cuts, downsizing, and the boss's kid getting your promotion after you've been with the company for thirty years.

I've had my share of real-life experiences.

I graduated from dental school in 1981 at age twenty-six. I bought a small practice in an Indiana farm town and started my practice that July. Within weeks of arriving to town, the local stock broker/financial advisor took me to lunch at a Pizza Hut. The conversation was mainly about setting up an IRA* account for my wife and me and included every line you could think of. "Time is on your side." "Start while you're young." "Just set aside a little bit each year and let compound interest do the rest." You've heard it all and could give this pitch yourselves.

*bubble: a state of booming economic activity (as in a stock market) that often ends in a sudden collapse

*IRA: An Individual Retirement Account (IRA) is a government sponsored, tax-deferred personal retirement plan.

1

So, I made an appointment for him to come to the house and sit down with us. He had a questionnaire for us to fill out so that he could go back and put in the numbers to run an evaluation for us. His first question was, "How much do you think you'll need in annual income when you retire?"

What?

I was twenty-six years old, just starting my business and I was completely baffled that he wanted me to give him some guessed-income amount for forty years from that point. He explained that he needed a number so that he could do the calculation, so I gave a random number to make him happy. But I thought it was strange.

There was a tax break involved, and the IRA contribution was only $2,000 per year each for my wife and me, so I contributed for three consecutive years. That was a total of $12,000. The early 80's were not the greatest times for investors. In fact, it was rather awful timing. But I was very busy trying to build my practice and paid no attention to that kind of thing.

I won't ever forget the day I sat at my desk and looked at the report laying out how my IRA investment was performing and its value after three years. It said, $11,600. After the brokerage fees, I actually lost $400 of my investment! So, I called the advisor to find out what was happening.

You know how that conversation went.

"The market will always go through these cycles. But you have nothing to worry about; time is on your side. It'll rally

2

back soon and go higher than ever. The market has gone through these corrections for over a hundred years."

Then I asked him the first thing that came to my mind. "What if this happens when I'm sixty-nine and not twenty-nine? What if there's a correction right at the time I need my money?" He didn't miss a beat: "That's what diversification is all about," he said. "By then we will have you all diversified and you'll be protected from all of this."

I knew nothing about investing, but I WAS raised in cattle country and knew very well what BS smelled like!

When I hung up the phone, I looked at the paper and decided that I was never going to be in a position where a "correction" was going to affect my life and what I wanted to do. I shredded the paper, threw it in the trash, and forgot about it. I went back to building my practice, but I knew there was no way that I was going to allow my future to be determined by factors outside of MY control.

Believe it or not, this type of process still goes on today. The calculations are much more "sophisticated," and the presentations are more aesthetically pleasing, but the concept is the same. You give a bunch of data on your ideal life and the computer gives you, "Your Number." This is the magic amount of money you will need to have set aside to be working for you when you no longer want to work, or just aren't able to. And, as long as there is no war, recession, depression, oil embargoes, terror attacks, bubbles, or stock market crashes, everything will be just fine.

I wish every single day was a stroll through the Magic Kingdom, but, I'm sorry this is Earth. This is life, and the odds of that working out are like going to Las Vegas and walking away with a million dollars. It has been done, but the odds are against you. So good luck...

It wasn't just a problem in the 80's. My brother is a broker and financial planner. About fifteen years ago, one of the senior partners at the firm where he was working retired. This partner had been in the business his whole life and decided that he had done a good job of planning and that the time was right. Now remember that last part.

My brother had a good relationship with him, and they would periodically have lunch together. However, around 2009/2010, the tone of their lunches changed. His friend was sincerely worried about running out of money. His investments had taken some major hits. He said his wife was still spending money like she did when he was working. She wanted to take the same nice vacations, have the same lifestyle, and she wasn't really in the mood to cut back, so he was in despair about what he was going to do. He had already surrendered all of his licenses and was backed into a corner.

Are you getting the significance of this? Here was a *trained career professional* who had reached "his number" and all of a sudden, retirement was stressful... and no fun!

I'm not trying to ruin your day, but someone has to start pointing out that this strategy has some major, mortal flaws. It really isn't any better than going to Vegas, betting your retirement account at the blackjack table, and ending up with nothing. Why is that considered irresponsible and reckless when rolling the dice with the current financial system is still considered prudent, logical, and accepted?

Don't worry; there is a better way.

There is a strategy that I have personally applied (and most people can also apply) that will allow you to *never* be put into this awful position. It has nothing to do with the DOW Jones Industrial Average,* prime interest rates, the price of gold, or who is in the White House.

I'm not claiming to be the first to have applied this strategy. I'm not claiming to have something revolutionary. I'm not trying to promote that you get in on the ground floor of anything. And, I'm not trying to sell you a particular product or service. I'm just trying to inspire you to think.

I've made my share of mistakes. Luckily though, I've always tried to learn something from them. And I never quit. That comes from a lot more than just being stubborn or trying to show everyone that I was right all along.

There really is a strategy that almost anyone can apply where you will love what you do, make a great living, and never want to retire.

My Philosophy:

If you love what you do, then you will never work a day in your life and have everything that you want.

DOW Jones Industrial Average*: the daily average of the stock prices of a group of large American companies.

I'm not trying to convince you, or anyone else, that you should change anything that you are currently doing. I'm not trying to get you to agree with me. But what I am trying to do is make you think for yourself and not just mindlessly follow the crowd over a cliff.

I got caught up in the last real estate bubble and it didn't make me feel any better that hundreds of thousands of other people lost their shirts along with me. I didn't feel any better that lots of people, much smarter than I am, made the same mistakes that I made. I followed the herd and it cost me too.

What I am very proud of, however, is that I landed on my feet by figuring out and applying what I'm sharing in this book. And now, I'm applying it bigger and better than ever before. I really am having the time of my life. And *there's no reason why you can't join me.*

I'm trying to get you to listen to that little voice inside your head when it says, "That doesn't sound right." I'm trying to get you to ask more questions and be sure that everything you are doing has a purpose for you and those around you. You have to recognize that you impact and affect many people in day-to-day living. Many people are counting on you. So, if *you* do better, then a lot of others do better with you.

It's my intention to create an exponentially positive impact on your life. I'm going to share a lot of stories from my life and what I've learned from them so that you can see, and achieve, an actual application rather than happy thoughts with no workability. Hopefully that will make these concepts more real to you and easier to apply.

I have no intention of being motivational. It's my intention to be real about what we all confront on a daily basis and how to not just deal with it, but to actually win. Just remember, when the people around you win, then you win.

My Philosophy:

If you know me, you win.

It's my intention that by knowing me, and us working together, you will have a better life and you will win. So, read this book, apply what's in it in a way that works for you, **and win!**

I will be sharing "My Philosophy" throughout this book. These are realizations that have evolved over the years through my life experiences. Hopefully they will help you create your own "My Philosophy."

It is not my intention for you to become me. It is my intention that you have your own realizations and make your own decisions as you read along. I suggest you write them down and use them to create your own personal rules of engagement for different situations in life.

I've found that once I have these rules that I have developed for myself, my decisions are made more quickly and with more certainty. I'm less likely to be swayed into doing things that I might later regret. My confidence goes up, and I stay true to my own goals.

If you know me, you win.

I've found it quite priceless.

I want that for you. I want you to have success in business, and I want it to be FUN! I want you to be able to treat your life like a game. And it's my intention that, after reading my book, it becomes easier for you to win.

Who knows, someday I might just throw a big party for all my winners!

If you would like help in applying the concepts that I am writing about, you can get a free PDF of exercises I have created to help you get more out of reading "FUN AT WORK."

Simply go to www.funatworkthebook.com for the download.

Fun at Work

1
Business Basics

***

"Your work is going to fill a large part of your life, and the only way to be truly satisfied is to do what you believe is great work. And the only way to do great work is to love what you do."

Steve Jobs, Co-Founder, Chairman and CEO, Apple

"Any time is a good time to start a company."

Ron Conway, Noted Startup Investor, SV Angel

"I knew that if I failed, I wouldn't regret that, but I knew the one thing I might regret is not trying."

Jeff Bezos, Amazon Founder and CEO

"The way to get started is to quit talking and start doing."

Walt Disney, Co-Founder, Disney

"What do you need to start a business? Three simple things: know your product better than anyone, know your customer, and have a burning desire to succeed."

Dave Thomas, Founder, Wendy's

Fun at Work

"It's hard to beat a person who never gives up."

Babe Ruth, Baseball Legend

***

There are so many factors that enter into running a business that it can often seem overwhelming e.g. hiring, accounting, marketing, sales, management, and motivation of staff, etc. It's enough to drive an owner crazy!

The most annoying thing is that all that stuff is usually not what the owner is interested in at all. I don't believe I've ever heard an entrepreneur say, "I started my own company because I really love HR! I just love hiring people." Or, "I started my company so I could do the books. I just love numbers!" Nope.

I have heard many say, "I'm really good at helping people with _____. "Or "I'm really good at making _____."

It's the actual producing of the product or service that gets us excited about starting a company. We have very creative ideas on how to better serve the public with what we have to offer. We then spend time, money, and energy on making the product/service better and better. We take classes on that and hire consultants to help us with it.

Here's the problem: there's so much more to running a business than just providing a great product or service, and that's where all the parts start to swirl around our heads. That's when things become no fun.

What, exactly, is the simple process that builds a company?

Management

Sell ⟶ Deliver

Get New Customers

This is pretty basic. Sell the product or service, deliver it, and get more people to sell and deliver to. Management's job is to organize everyone and hold the machine together. So, the better you sell, deliver, promote, and organize, the more money you should make to sell, deliver, and promote even more.

During prosperity, you can get away with not putting a lot of attention on these things or not doing them very well. During a recession, those who know how to do these four things will survive, and probably prosper, and those that don't may go out of business. That's free enterprise.

You may think that this is too simple of a concept for me to even spend the time to write it or for you to read it, but

I have spoken with tens of thousands of business owners over the years and there are a few common mistakes made by a majority of them.

They find a part of being in business that they really like and then they ride that hobbyhorse* for all it's worth.

Some focus heavily on the product or service. All of their attention and resources go into making the delivery of the product/service <u>perfect</u>. They have the idea that if they build a better mousetrap, the world will come running. They invest heavily in equipment, software, highly skilled staff etc., all with the goal to outmaneuver the competition by just being better and having the better product.

The problem here is that if they aren't marketing or selling their awesome product, they go broke tinkering,* trying to make the perfect product/service. These owners usually have an engineering type of mind and they really enjoy product development. So, they justify their actions by saying that if they are the best, they can't help but succeed. Unfortunately, not so.

They also ignore management and believe they can always simply out-produce, or out-sell any problem. Maybe this will work for a short period of time, but it stunts the growth of the company.

*Hobbyhorse: a topic to which one constantly reverts, or continues to act on
*Tinkering: to repair, adjust, or experiment with

Another common mistake:

"Nobody in the company can do _____ as well as I can."

That's similar to the last mistake, but imagine it being said with tremendous pride, or tremendous despair. I'm going to cover more of this in the chapter, "Creating a Dynasty That Lasts for Decades or More." For now, let's just say that any basic function of the company that revolves around the owner is the area that will stop the growth of the company.

It's common to find a successful company where the owner is the best sales rep they have, and that's how it should be. But if there are no other sales reps, or the ones employed are ineffective, then the company has no chance of growing beyond what the owner can sell.

There are lots of things that I'm good at. I really like to execute those functions, but I'm always looking for my replacement. This isn't because I get tired of doing any one thing, but simply because of this main point: Any part of the company that relies completely on me will be the area of the company that stunts our growth.

Another mistake is:

Focusing on just one of these items and ignoring the others.

"If we could just handle _____, we would crush it!" Now everyone in the company is constantly focused on that until a fire breaks out in another part of the company. Then everyone rushes over to handle that area.

There are more mistakes that I could note, and there really are an infinite number of specific examples that we could compile and discuss about the problems that can arise when owning and managing a business. Instead...

What's the solution? The balancing act of walking across Niagara Falls on a tightwire.

All of these four areas of the company must be worked on concurrently. Naturally, depending on the business cycle you are in at any particular time, one of these is more important than the others. But you can't ignore the others.

Watch a professional walk a tightwire. Go look one up on YouTube right now and observe how many corrections they make every second. At any second, one correction is more important than another; but if they don't keep paying attention on the left side while they adjust to the right, they fall off.

Creating and running a successful business is a balancing act of promotion, sales, delivery, and management. They must all be worked on, and maintained, in order for the company to survive.

If I were to ask you which of these is *most* important, what would your answer be? We could actually make a case for each of these items.

Without promotion, there's no one to sell to. Without sales, we don't move any products or services. If our delivery sucks, then no one will buy or recommend us later. If our management is awful, then customers and employees are upset.

Now let's evaluate this. If there are no sales, then there is NO MONEY, and without money, the company doesn't survive. The truth is that you can actually suck at everything else; but if you can sell, you will keep the doors open. There will be enough money to make up for the inefficiencies and deficiencies of the other three.

The fact is that the Sales Department *is* the tightwire.

Without the tightwire, we have no tightwire act. It can't be more basic than this. Without sales, there is no company. So, if you are going to err in overemphasizing any of these, make it Sales.

Watch an episode of *Shark Tank*. Each new entrepreneur is cordially greeted. There are usually lots of smiles and joking that go back and forth with many questions about how the product works and the problem it solves.

However, watch how all the joking stops and the sharks stop smiling when one of them asks, "What are your sales?" The answer to that question determines if there will be a deal or a disappointed walk back down the hallway.

If the sales are great, I've seen the sharks fight over that deal. If the sales are poor, no one is interested.

This is not a book on Sales. I'll save that for another day. However, the point is that if you can't sell, then you should go work for someone else; but if you *can* sell, you can't ignore any of these four items. If you aren't good at something, hire someone who is.

This next item is critical.

My Philosophy:

> **Whatever you are doing, do it FAST!**

***

"Waiting for perfect is never as smart as making progress."

Seth Godin, Author

"If everything seems under control, you're just not going fast enough."

Mario Andretti, Legendary Race Car Driver

***

No matter what industry or service, all other factors being equal, I can generally say that the company that can deliver the product or service faster will be the one that wins. I realize that quality can't be sacrificed in the interest of speed, but let's take a look at this.

Do you like waiting? I don't. If all factors are equal, I'm going where I can get the product or service faster.

**Whatever you are doing,
do it FAST!**

McDonald's put the fast into fast food. Look at how they have been copied.

There's also Amazon. They are dominating on convenience and speed alone.

Look at Uber. I can usually get a ride in less than five minutes. If I'm in a remote location and I ask someone to call a taxi, I'd have to wait thirty minutes or more. Taxi companies can complain about Uber all day long, but they were just never worried enough about servicing the public *faster,* and someone really smart figured out how to do it.

In dentistry, it's common for certain procedures to have to be sent to a dental laboratory to make the restoration that will fix the tooth.

A crown is one of the more common procedures that requires this. It is made out of metal or porcelain that goes around the tooth and holds it together when there has been a large cavity or filling. It is usually done in two steps: the first step is to remove any decay and old filling, take an impression* and make a temporary crown* so the tooth is protected while waiting on the final restoration to be made. The second step is to cement the crown into place.

*Impression: imprint of hard (teeth) and soft tissues in the mouth from which a positive reproduction (cast or model) can be formed.

*Crown: In dentistry, the crown of a tooth refers to the visible area, usually covered by enamel. Therefore, synthetically made Crowns are used most commonly to entirely cover a damaged tooth or cover an implant.

The typical wait time is two to three weeks while the dental lab makes the crown, but I negotiated with my lab to get my crowns to me in seven to ten days. My fees were about 25% higher than other dentists in the area, but I delivered faster and I felt that made me worth it. So did a lot of the patients in my area.

There is a machine today that many dentists have that eliminates the need to make a crown in two visits. The dentist prepares the tooth, takes a digital photograph of the tooth, and sends it to a machine that grinds out the crown in eight minutes. The crown is then cemented to the tooth.

That machine costs $125,000, and they sell a lot of them.

Why? Because a smart person figured out how to reduce the time of getting a crown into the patient's mouth from three weeks to eight minutes. Brilliant!

When patients came to my practice, they didn't wait. If we were ever ten minutes behind schedule, we knew that we had to move our butts and get back on schedule. Wouldn't you pay a little bit more for that kind of service from your doctors?

We organized our schedule so that we didn't run behind. My fees were higher, and that is one of the reasons I felt we were worth it. No waiting.

Now let's talk about quality. You absolutely can't turn out a product or service that sucks. If so, the advantage that you gain in speed is lost. You can't, however, sacrifice speed in the interest of perfection.

And here is that damn tightwire walk again. If you focus too much on quality at the sacrifice of speed, you lose. If you focus too much on speed at the sacrifice of quality, you lose.

So, the company that can best balance speed and quality in the four basics of business will win. It's too simple. Do things fast and do them right.

If you pull that off, you will constantly grow and overtake your competition.

You may think that I'm only interested in expansion, that I'm one of those guys that is never satisfied with the existing level of production, or that I constantly push to grow no matter how well we are doing.

You're right! Is there any other way to survive in business? The moment you get complacent and are just happy with the status quo, you are vulnerable. You are vulnerable to acts of Congress increasing taxes or regulations in your industry; acts of Mother Nature like blizzards, tornadoes, floods, and hurricanes; acts of life like having a key staff member move out of the area, auto accidents and severe illness. The possibilities are endless.

In physics, there is a Law of Natural Decay. If not acted upon, anything in this universe will naturally tend to decay.

You can drive a brand-new Mercedes home, park it in the garage, and if you let it sit there for fifty years, it will be a piece of worthless junk.

This applies to cars, houses, food, bodies, and businesses.

You always need to be thinking about how to expand and take on more territory. However, that expansion has to be balanced with what? Profit. (More on this later with its own chapter) Lean too far in one direction and you aren't going to make it.

There is a difference between being self-employed and being a CEO.

The self-employed can make a good living by working for themselves and delivering a quality product/service. They have the benefits of being their own boss and determining their own schedule etc.

The disadvantage is that they often make the same amount of money, or less, than if they did the same thing for someone else; usually, while working more hours. That's the trade off, and not an ideal situation.

They can make a good living and have a nice lifestyle, which is fine if that's the goal, but I think it's a bit risky. What if something happens to the owner? It could doom the company.

Instead, I think it's best to evolve into a CEO. The CEO can inspire and lead others to get these four things done. The CEO doesn't even consider doing all the work.

Can you imagine the CEO of GM down on the assembly line making a car? Unthinkable!

Can you imagine them on a lot selling a car? Ridiculous!

Can you imagine them in front of a computer all day laying out the script of the next Super Bowl ad? You're fired!

If you want to have a successful business, you must learn how to balance all of these things on a daily, weekly, monthly and annual basis.

That's the tightwire walk of any business owner and CEO.

If you would like help in applying the concepts that I am writing about, you can get a free PDF of exercises I have created to help you get more out of reading "FUN AT WORK."

Simply go to www.funatworkthebook.com for the download.

2

Money: Good Versus Evil

Every game has to have a prize to go after. The NFL has the Super Bowl and the Vince Lombardi Trophy,* the NHL has the Stanley Cup, and the Olympics have gold medals. Games have trophies, prizes and rewards.

We can all picture the Super Bowl winning team standing on a podium in the center of a stadium being awarded the Vince Lombardi Trophy. The confetti is coming down and the stage is crowded with players, coaches, owners, and media personalities all trying to share in the glory of a well-played game.

Many times, we even see these grown men cry with joy. The fans go crazy and party well into the wee hours of the morning. Why is that? It's just a piece of metal.

That piece of metal represents something. It represents accomplishment, self-satisfaction, bragging rights, future income, a legacy and many other things. It represents something different to every player, coach, owner, and fan, but it also represents the same thing to everyone: a *winner*.

I've had the chance to personally experience this as a fan. In 1976, my Indiana Hoosiers* won the NCAA basketball tourney.* To this day, they are the last

*Vince Lombardi Trophy: The Vince Lombardi Trophy is the trophy awarded each year to the winning team of the National Football League's championship game, the Super Bowl. The trophy is named in honor of NFL coach Vince Lombardi, who led the Green Bay Packers to victories in the first two Super Bowl games.

undefeated team to have come out on top during March Madness. It was an unbelievable thrill to be in the third row for those two games of the Final Four and share in that moment.

My Green Bay Packers have won Super Bowls. My favorite race car drivers have won NASCAR championships. My favorite golfers have won major tournaments. And when we win, we always feel great!

We all look back at the hard work of the players, parents, and everyone associated with the winning organizations with such a feeling of satisfaction, pride, and amazement. And everyone agrees that, whatever that sacrifice was, it was all worth it in the end.

So, what is generally the prize in the game of life?

Money

It may not specifically be money, but the prize in the game of life is to accumulate enough possessions that represent money as one can, i.e. property, stocks and bonds, precious metal and gems, etc. The more you accumulate, the bigger the win, the greater the freedom and security and the more control you have over your future.

We sacrifice a lot to win this game. We spend time away

*Indiana Hoosiers: A Hoosier is a native or inhabitant of Indiana (used as a nickname). The Indiana Hoosiers are the intercollegiate sports teams and players of Indiana University Bloomington. In this work, the author refers to the 1976 Men's Basketball Team who won the NCAA tournament after an undefeated season.

*tourney: tournament

from our families and put in long hours for our own business or for our employers. We spend money on education. We take risks that can have long-term consequences if we lose. All this for the ultimate prize of money and what it represents to each of us.

But how many times have you seen someone who has won it all and is still miserable?

They end up divorced with their families torn apart. They become addicted to drugs or alcohol and lose everything that they worked so hard to accomplish. They build a huge company and lose it all. And what about the lottery winner who in five or ten years is right back to where they started? Or worse.

We have all seen someone whose personality completely changed when they acquired lots of money. They are no longer close with their friends and family. They become rude, arrogant, and dismissive of those that have helped them along the way.

We often see people seemingly win the game of life and lose *everything* else. We, and sometimes they, stand back and ask, "Was it really worth it?"

I have a question:

Do we have money or does money have us?

Doesn't money influence everything we do? What time we get out of bed. Where we live. What we eat. What we drive. Where our kids go to school. And everything else?

Many have come to believe that money is evil. Sure, we can make a long list of destructive things that some folks have done with their money.

But wait a minute. What about all the people that *help* others with their money?

They start charitable organizations, feed the hungry, house the homeless, build hospitals and add buildings onto universities. There are so many heart-warming stories.

Each of us can look back on times in our lives where we gave our hard-earned dollars away to a cause that meant something to us, and we felt great about it! Even if it meant that we weren't going to be able to have or do something for ourselves. We felt great that we were able to do something for someone else that they weren't able to do for themselves.

So here is the bottom line: *money is just money*. It doesn't talk or walk or do anything on its own. It's actually just a piece of paper with ink on it. It inherently has no more power and influence than a grain of sand on the beach. It's simply a tool in the game of life.

So, what's the game here?

My Philosophy:

People can use money to create, and people can use money to destroy.

Money is not the problem. People are. Money is not the solution. People are. Money doesn't do bad or good. People do.

People can use money to create and people can use money to destroy.

What is it then that determines if a person is going to do good or do bad? Does it have to do with how they were raised? Where they were born? Who influenced them? To a certain degree, yes; but, each of us has a free will to make our own decisions. We all get to decide if we are going to create or destroy.

There are many stories of individuals who have had all the odds stacked against them. There is no way they should have been able to survive in their environment or circumstances; yet, they persisted and succeeded.

I personally know a quadriplegic* who has donated hundreds of thousands of dollars to charity. He has more challenges than I have ever had, but he is one of the happiest people I know.

What, then, is the determining factor? Well, it's simply a matter of what game a person decides to play. Are they playing a game to win by destroying others, or are they playing a game to win by helping others?

A drug dealer is playing a game to win by destroying others. That's pretty obvious. And the game is about making money, lots and lots of money! It doesn't matter how many lives are destroyed and how many people die.

Just as long as the drug dealer makes money and accumulates power to make more money and destroy more.

*quadriplegic: permanently unable to move or feel your arms or legs, usually because of a severe injury to the spine

Pablo Escobar was one of the most famous and rich drug dealers of all time. He lived in Colombia and had influence over government officials and police from the early 70's until his death in 1993. It is estimated that he was responsible for 80% of the cocaine brought into the U.S. during that time.

He had so much money that he didn't know what to do with all of it. He was hiding it in houses and burying it in the ground in secret locations. At one point, his drug organization was making more money than General Motors. Basically, he had more money than he could ever spend.

However, the more money he made, the more people he destroyed. Did he really win? He couldn't live where he wanted to live because the police and military would find him. And what about his competition? They were also trying to kill him so they could have his territory and resources.

He couldn't travel where he wanted to travel because it wasn't safe, and he definitely couldn't do whatever he wanted to do. Money supposedly represents all kinds of freedom and power, but in the end, ultimate wealth made and kept him a prisoner. He destroyed everything around him. Eventually, he lost his life in a gunfight with the Colombian police and military surrounding him.

Pablo Escobar was obviously a very smart and creative man. The organization that he put together can, on some levels, be admired. He had manufacturing facilities, a sales force and international distribution centers. He was very well known and quite popular among the citizens until near the end of his reign. Some called him a genius, but he used his creative genius to destroy. It's impossible to calculate how many lives he destroyed and how many died. We can think of other such personalities all throughout history.

That's a pretty extreme case of destruction. Let's look at a case of incredible creation.

Walt Disney affected the lives of so many people on earth in ways that very few ever have. He was born in 1901 and was raised in Kansas City. His family was not wealthy, so he had a paper route when he was nine that he ran for six years. When he got older, his dad wanted him to work in a factory, but he wanted to be an artist. So, he started his own company and went bankrupt when he was twenty-one. Later, when asked about this, he said that he thought it was important to have a good, fine failure when you're young.

Unfazed, he headed out to Hollywood. He was unemployed, but he had a dream of having his own animation studio. He and his brother opened the first animated cartoon studio in town, yet, a few years later he was headed for his second bankruptcy.

It was at that exact point when Mickey Mouse went from a vision in his head onto a piece of paper. He said that the purpose of Mickey was to make people laugh. The first animation starring Mickey Mouse, "Plane Crazy," was released in 1928 when Walt was twenty-seven.

In 1932, he won the first Oscar ever given to a cartoon for his "Flowers and Trees" short story in color. That ended up being the first of his twenty-six Academy Awards. It took him two years to produce *Snow White*, which was a huge hit and he used all the profits, plus borrowed another $500,000, to build his own studio in 1938.

By that time, he had so many projects going that if one failed, the next successful one was right around the corner. *Cinderella* was a huge hit, but then he turned around and lost money on *Alice in Wonderland*. *Mary Poppins* was released in 1964 and cost Walt ten million dollars to make. That is the equivalent of *eighty million dollars today!* And he had no evidence that people were going to like it because nothing like it had ever been made.

He got the idea for Disneyland while taking his kids around to different animal parks and amusement attractions. While they were on roller coasters, he was dreaming of how he could make a bigger impact by creating an ideal environment where people could visit and enjoy a day with their families and friends.

He said of Disney World, "It will never cease to be a living blueprint of the future. Where people actually live a life, they can't find anywhere else in the world."

Walt tells a story of a little boy asking him questions late in his career. The lad was inquiring if Walt still drew Mickey, and he admitted that he didn't. The boy asked if he still did the animations, and Walt said he didn't. Then the youngster asked, "Well, what is it that you do then?"

Walt replied, "I think of myself as a little bee. I go from one area of the studio to another and gather pollen and sort of stimulate everybody. I guess that's the job I do."

He went on to say, "After forty-some odd years in the business, my greatest reward is, I think, is I've been enabled to build this wonderful organization. Also, to have the public appreciate and accept what I've done all these years. That, that is a great reward." (To listen to the entire interview with him go to *The Walt Disney Story* on YouTube)

Today, one hundred seventy-five million people visit Disney attractions all over the world every year. That represents roughly 2.5% of the world's population. That doesn't even include everyone who watches a Disney film or buys a Disney book yearly. It's impossible to calculate how much of the world's population his creative genius impacts every year. Even decades since he has passed away, it's hard to determine how many people he is still making smile.

I believe we can safely say that Pablo Escobar and Walt Disney couldn't represent greater polar opposites when it comes down to a person deciding what they are going to do with their life.

What then is at the foundation of whether someone is going to create or destroy? What is the foundation of whether a business will be around for days or generations? What really is at the core of winning the game of life or losing? Is it actually money, or something else?

If you would like help in applying the concepts that I am writing about, you can get a free PDF of exercises I have created to help you get more out of reading "FUN AT WORK." Simply go to www.funatworkthebook.com for the download.

Fun at Work

3

Life Must Have a Basic Purpose

This will be the longest chapter in the book because I consider it to contain the most important information. This is the data that determines every decision that I make, and every action that I take. I attribute *all* of my success to this concept. So, read this chapter over and over and over again until you can say, "I got it."

What made Pablo Escobar and Walt Disney polar opposites was their purpose in life.

Escobar had the purpose to make money and accumulate power no matter the cost. No matter who he destroyed. He was more interested in helping himself than helping others.

Disney had the purpose to make people smile and give them an experience unlike anywhere else on Earth. He put helping others ahead of helping himself. He held this purpose so high that he went bankrupt once, and routinely risked his entire fortune to achieve it.

At some point, each of them had a decision to make, and the results of each of their decisions are obvious to all of us. We all have had to make these kinds of decisions that determine whether our future will be good or bad.

I want to share a couple of my personal stories as examples of this.

Around the time I was fourteen or fifteen, these were the questions I asked myself. "What am I going to be? What do I like to do? How do I want my life to play out?"

I was the student trainer for the basketball team, and I was having a lot of fun with that. I enjoyed helping the athletes recover and play through their injuries. The school even sent me to a week-long training program at the University of Miami of Ohio. That was a really cool experience for a high school freshman.

What I liked the most about being a student trainer was that I felt like I was a vital part of the team. I got to be in the team photos, ride on the team bus, and hang out with the guys. I definitely wasn't good enough to play, but I got to help keep the good players playing. I taped up their sprained ankles, got out of class to put them in the whirlpool, and treated their injuries. I was actually pretty good at it. I read books and always tried to learn more about how I could keep everyone playing at peak performance. To top it off, they were also my friends, so it was a blast.

I knew that I was definitely going to go to Indiana University. I found out that they had a great program for athletic trainers, so that was on my list of possible careers.

My dad came up to me one day and said he had run into our family dentist who asked him what I was going to do with my life. My dad told him that I wasn't sure, so he suggested that I consider becoming a dentist.

Now, I have to admit that I was not the ideal dental patient. I didn't go twice a year to have my teeth cleaned and examined, and I had proven to be not very diligent about watching the sugar I consumed either because I'd had several cavities.

It honestly wasn't a profession that was on my radar. I mean, who wants to give people shots in their mouth and drill on teeth?!

But the dentist offered to let me come and observe him working on a Saturday morning to get an idea of what it was like. I wasn't all that excited about it, but I thought I should at least check it out as an option before deciding against it. I'll also admit that he lived in a nice house and drove a Cadillac, so that got my attention.

A few weeks later I took him up on his offer.

I won't go into the details, but while I watched him work and listened to him explain everything he was doing, I became really intrigued. It was quite fascinating how a patient would show up with a broken tooth or cavity and he would fix it right up for them. He was *really* helping them! Dentistry got added to my list of possible career choices.

When he was done treating patients, we sat down, and he explained the process of getting a dental degree. I would have to get a four-year degree in some subject like biology, chemistry, etc. (and I really didn't like that stuff all that much). Then I would have to apply for a dental school, get accepted, and put in four more years to get my dental degree. That was a bit of a shocker. We are talking about eight more years of school after high school graduation before I could open a practice.

A concern we both shared was that our small local high school—enrollment of four hundred students in four grades—didn't have any college preparatory level courses in chemistry, biology or anything else that would help me when I got to college. Needless to say, it was going to be an academic challenge. I was a pretty good student, but there were many in my class who were smarter than I was.

What I decided to do was go to IU, take all of the pre-dental classes, and see if I could get admitted. Those prerequisites would also cover me if I wanted to become an athletic trainer. I had a starting point. All I had to do now was get to work.

I have to tell you that my first semester at IU was pretty brutal. First of all, there were about as many students in my dormitory quad as there were in my hometown. Then, I couldn't see my girlfriend every day like I had for four years. The courses were very hard, and the dorm food bore no resemblance to my mom's home cooking. Drugs were readily available, and many on my dorm floor had no hesitation in using them. It was a definite culture shock.

I won't get into all the bloody details, but it was really hard. One of my friends from high school flunked out at the end of the first year, and another one quit at the end of the second year. I had to hire a tutor just to get a C in Organic Chemistry. To top it off, I even broke up with my high school sweetheart.

The only thing that kept me going was pursuing the goal of becoming an athletic trainer or a dentist. I really wanted to do something worthwhile and both of those professions interested me.

After surviving my first year in college, I found out that a local star athlete had just gotten into dental school. I talked to him and we arranged for me to get a tour of the IU dental school after the holiday break. That visit to the dental school ended up being the real turning point.

Here was someone I knew, doing what I wanted to do, and it looked so great to be able to do it. *Really* helping people with something that very few in America are trained to do. It became real to me that I could do this—if I could just get accepted.

I became more determined to go to dental school. Becoming an athletic trainer had fallen from being a viable option to just being my emergency parachute if I couldn't get into dental school. I studied my ass off, but it wasn't easy, and I spent a lot of time at the library and studied late into many nights.

Obviously, I got in. There were one hundred thirty positions for eleven hundred applicants. I felt blessed.

Then, just to add to the fun, the first semester of dental school was harder than my first semester at IU. I never in a million years could have imagined how demanding it was. One classmate had been in the Army and said dental school was even harder than boot camp—especially because it lasted for four years. A couple of my classmates quit in the first year and the dental school dismissed five more after the second year for various reasons. Somehow, I still graduated and got my license.

Finally, I opened my office, but then I ran into a whole new set of challenges right up to the point where after eleven years in practice, I was considering laying off half the staff, reducing my hours, and going to work part-time for someone else so I could pay my bills.

So, what's the point of me going into all of this? To try to impress you with how awesome I am? Not at all. The point here is that if you have a purpose that you believe in, you will literally go through hell to achieve it. I wasn't the smartest, the prettiest, or the most athletic, but I was very determined to get that dental degree; and I got it. I was determined to succeed in private practice, and I did it. I had to persist and figure it out.

And *you* can achieve anything you want to as well. Uh Oh! Here we go into all that self-help mantra about, "how much potential you have and that you can achieve anything."

I tried a bunch of that stuff by the self-help gurus and found most of it quite empty and not helpful. I read the books, bought the audio and video training programs, and heard many of them lecture in person. I was always looking for some magic solution or the quick hit that would take all the pressure off of me.

And after decades of pushing to achieve my goals, I have concluded that success depends heavily on:

My Philosophy:

Deciding to help a lot of people by doing something that you like. Then work hard!

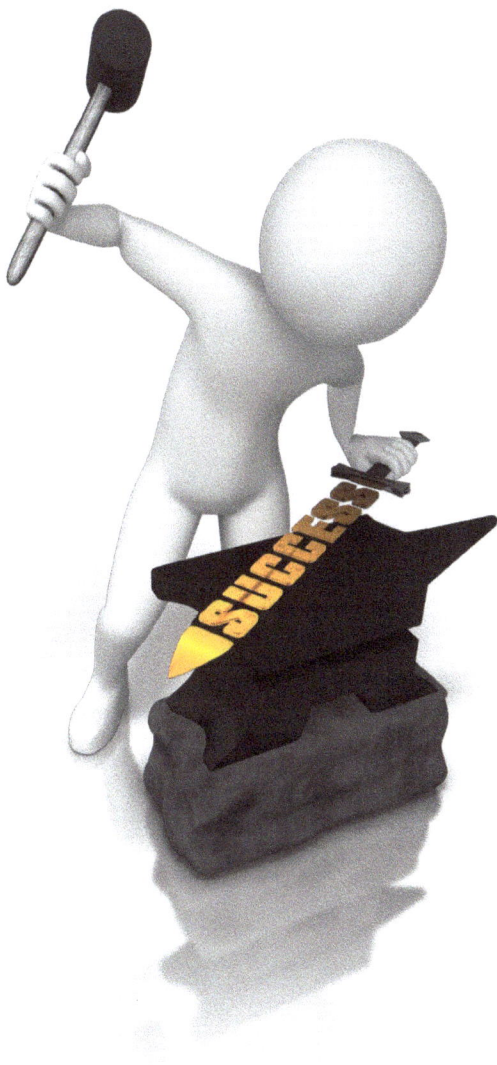

Decide to help a lot of people by doing something you like.

Then work hard!

The harder you work and the more people you help, the more time and money you'll get to help more people by doing what you like to do. It's a never-ending, perpetual game.

A very close friend of mine was offered an early retirement package, so of course he took it. He and his wife were staying with us for a week soon after that. During their stay, he asked me when I was going to retire. With no hesitation I said "Never! I don't work now! I love what I do so much that I would rather do this than golf. I plan on living to at least a hundred, and I'm never going to stop helping people."

That wasn't a planned response, but it just rolled off my tongue because that's how I live. I have a great life! Is it always easy? Nope. Does everything always magically go my way? Nope. Do all of my ideas go right and win? Nope. I've lost a lot of money on many of my ideas, but I never quit trying to help more people with my next idea.

I help a lot of people. I love what I do, so I never work a day in my life—although I often go to bed late and wake up early, putting in sixty to eighty-hour weeks. Here's the thing though, I have everything that I want. My life is a huge game and I love playing it with all my friends.

Take it from a guy who has done it right and done it wrong. There is one powerful concept that determines *everything* in your life. That is your answer to the questions:

"What's your goal?" "What's your purpose?"

"What's the mission statement of your company?"

"Who are you going to help and how?"

This all equates to your Basic Purpose.

The key point here is that you MUST FOCUS OUTWARD when stating what your goal is. If you say, "my goal is to become a millionaire," your focus is on yourself. I have no problem with you making a million dollars a year. But that isn't going to happen unless you first focus on helping enough people get what they want, or need, who then pay you that million dollars.

My Philosophy:

Your Basic Purpose is *not* about you. It's about others.

**The more people you help, the
more money you will make.**

Here's the best way to look at it:

How much money you make is just a reflection of how many people you are helping and to what magnitude. It's like the scoreboard in an athletic contest. You can help a ton of people a little bit for a small fee and make a million dollars, or you can help a few people a lot for a large fee and make a million dollars.

But if you're running around worried about how to make a million dollars, and you haven't figured out who you're going to help and how, **then be prepared to fail**. If you are just going after the rich people so you can make a lot of money, your odds are better in Las Vegas. They will smell

**The more people you help,
the more money you will make.**

you coming a mile away and have their butler or security guard escort you off their estate.

I don't think I can state this any more clearly. Figure out who you are going to help before you start planning how you're going to spend your first million dollars. Also, if you love what you're doing as you help them, then you just made a million dollars doing what you love. And had a lot of FUN!

I mentioned earlier that I didn't grow up wanting to be a dentist. I wasn't all that excited about it when my dad first mentioned that he talked to our dentist, but when I investigated it, I loved the concept of someone having a major problem and my being able to *help* them.

Then I went to the dental school with my friend and got a better idea of what a dentist does. I was more interested. Then I found out that people with teeth live longer than people without teeth, and I was hooked. After that, I wanted to become the best dentist I could be so that I could help people live longer.

That Basic Purpose has influenced every decision I have made since that moment.

I was driven to get more continuing education so I could help my patients more and more. I spent a lot of money on courses and equipment that others were more unwilling to buy, and I left my family to travel around the country so that I could study and train with the best. All so I could make more money? Hell No!! So, I could help people live longer.

Have I sometimes strayed from helping others? Hell yes! I'm far from perfect. I have another story or two that I think you will find very interesting. But I've always snapped out of it and gotten back on track to helping people solve their problems.

I have an exercise that might just help you figure this out for yourself. No one can do it for you. All you have to do is answer the following questions. I suggest you write down your answers.

Questions:

1. Who can you help with a product or service?
2. How old are they?
3. Where do they live?
4. Describe them in detail.
5. How many of them are there?
6. What problem will it help them solve? Describe it precisely.
7. Why would they buy it from you and not someone else? You must distinguish the product and service from the competition. Are you faster, more durable, higher quality, cheaper? There has to be something.

You need to know the answers to these questions. Use the internet to find out everything you can about your target group of people. Then go talk to them and find out exactly what their problem is and how you think you could help them solve it. See if they like your ideas. Get their feedback and figure it out *with them*, not just in your own head.

Here's the final question, and possibly the one you wanted to ask earlier; but you can't ask it before you have the answer to the others. Can they afford it? I saved this question until the end because it doesn't need to be asked until now. It really is the least important of the questions; but it's the one that is usually asked first or second.

"How much money can we make?" can easily end up making you focus on yourself in a heartbeat. And you will find yourself flying into a black hole, possibly never to be seen or heard from again.

Also keep this in mind. I hate seeing Cheaper as an answer to question #7. The race to be cheapest is a race to the bottom of the ocean and there can be only *one* cheapest. So, if you're competing on price, you will usually lose. Notice that even the almighty Walmart has had its problems focusing on prices. Cheapest is not an easy road to success.

Please don't go down that path.

I don't watch much television. About the only thing that I watch is ESPN and movies, but one of my favorite shows is *Shark Tank*.

It's real, because the investors are using their own money and they ask lots and lots of questions. All of the questions are basically designed to find out: 1) does it really help people, 2) if it does, then how many have you helped so far and 3) are you making enough money to warrant me working with you to help a lot more people.

Ask yourself tons of questions. I gave you a list just to get you started, just come up with an idea and pretend you're on *Shark Tank*. Be real about it.

The solution here is to find out what problem you can help someone solve, and then design the product and service to solve it. Then factor in a profit for yourself and that's your price. If it really is faster, more durable, higher quality, and longer lasting, then you can pretty much charge what the market will bear because you are helping people solve a problem. Discounts are for those who can't close, but I'll save that discussion for another book and another day.

If you look online, you'll see you can buy a vacuum cleaner for anywhere between $50 and $1,000 dollars. Can you see that a $50 vacuum cleaner solves a different problem than a $1,000 vacuum cleaner?

What about the hotel/motel business? For example, we have Motel 6, Holiday Inn, Hilton, and the Ritz Carlton. They range in price for a night in New York City from $70 to $725 for a basic room. Each of these establishments solves a different problem for different kinds of customers, and they must be doing it pretty well because they are all still open for business. They know what their purpose is and how to fill the need of their customers while still making a profit.

This is a broad statement that will not apply to every situation and every business.

My Philosophy:

A business that is struggling to expand or survive has lost its Basic Purpose or never had one in the first place.

I'd like to make this concept a bit more real by running through an example using fictitious characters. I wouldn't be surprised if something like this hasn't already happened to you. Just imagine a friend giving you this get-rich pitch.

Roger has always been after the next get-rich scheme. He has pitched me on more ground floor projects than I can count. Here's his latest one.

Roger likes to fish. He recently went to Canada for a week with his usual friends, but there was a new guy, Nigel, there. He seemed to be rather wealthy, smart, and everybody liked him. While sitting around the campfire one evening, Nigel started to tell the group about his latest idea.

Worm Farms.

Roger's voice started to get higher as he began describing this amazing opportunity.

Everybody LOVES to fish. And EVERYBODY knows that worms are the fish's favorite food. One of the problems with worms, however, is that they cost money and they are hard to keep alive. Nigel has solved both problems. He has devised a way to grow worms by the billions and he has a new life-support system for worms that will keep them alive for a month. Nigel is a freaking genius!!

He has done all his research on his forty acres in North Carolina for the past three years perfecting his techniques. He's tried to do this elsewhere in America, but there's a particular enzyme in the ground on his property that the worms eat up like filet mignon. It's like steroids for worms! While scouring America, he has found that this enzyme only exists in his county.

His plan is to secure four hundred acres in his county. A wealthy landowner just died, and his widow has no idea what the property is worth, so he thinks he can get it for half of what it would normally cost. Now that's even better for *us* because that will do nothing but increase the profits on his conservative projections.

He originally was going to keep this opportunity for just his family and closest friends, but the banks think that this is too speculative. Stupid bankers! He really wants to take this big. Overnight!

And that's why he's offering this opportunity now to only, friends of friends. Roger was so lucky to have been on this fishing trip! According to him, all we have to do is get forty people to put up $50,000 each to get the property and start growing worms. And do you want to know the best part? The worms are already in the ground! All we have to do is install his patent-pending worm corrals, to keep our investment from wandering off the property, and we will be in business overnight!

Now Roger saved the best part for last. The return on our investment is conservatively estimated to be 1,000:1!!!!! That's fifty million apiece for the original investors! He spared sharing with me the more real projection of profits because that would be too unbelievable.

Roger had gone home and gotten a third mortgage on his house and gathered up every penny that he could find. The problem is that he only had twenty-five thousand dollars. Now, because he likes me so much, he was willing to split a share with me if I would pitch in the other twenty-five thousand dollars. This really was an opportunity of a lifetime for me.

Roger and I grew up fishing as kids, and the one thing I knew for sure is that Roger *hated* worms. He always fished with artificial bait because he couldn't stand the slimy live bait. When I asked him about that, he didn't miss a beat and said, "Of course, I still hate worms! But I'll *eat* the damn things for breakfast, lunch, and dinner for fifty million dollars!"

Needless to say, I passed up this opportunity of a lifetime. First of all, it was all about the money. Secondly, I didn't know the players in the game, and from the sound of it, everyone saw this as a money grab. So, I'm not interested.

As Roger walked away, he assured me that his phone would be on if I changed my mind.

Roger got his stepbrother, Pat, to give him the other twenty-five thousand dollars. I didn't hear much from them for about a year or so, but I do remember my wife telling me, however, that he and his wife had to move in with Pat and his family when they lost their house.

I saw Roger at a family reunion about a year and a half after our first conversation, so I asked him how the worm farm was working out. He just hung his head.

Nigel got the two million dollars from his forty investors and bought the property. The only problem was that he put the deed in his wife's name. Then he divorced his wife and bankrupted the company. He and his now ex-wife built a new house on the four hundred acres and bought an airplane for the private landing strip he had installed on the land.

It was obvious that Nigel's plan all along was to find forty people he could take advantage of by selling them on get-rich quick scheme and work it out administratively so that he and his wife could get the property for free and have a great life. This type of thing, sadly, happens all too often.

It's easy to feel sorry for Roger. He was a good guy and just trying to make a living. He had a dead-end job that barely paid the bills. He and his wife worked nights and weekends in their second jobs to keep two kids in college. He was really doing the best that he could.

(Let's apply the exercise I just suggested to you to see if we can help Roger. I'll ask the questions.)

Me: "What are you really good at?"

Roger: "Nothing!"

I knew he was a really good hunter. Nobody I knew could get a hunting license, leave the house the next morning at 4 a.m., and be cleaning a deer in his garage four hours later. This happened year after year after year. And he loved it! He lived for deer season. Others would take him hunting just so they were assured of getting their deer in less than nine days of 4 AM hunts.

I tried another approach: "What do you love to do?"

Roger: "Hunt."

Me: "I hear you're pretty good at it."

Roger: "None better."

Me: "OK. Have you ever helped anybody hunt?"

Roger: "Tons of people?"

Me: "Great. Tell me about the type of person you've helped hunt."

Roger: "Well, most of them enjoy hunting, but they don't know anything about how animals think. I've studied where they go. What their habits are. I just know where to find them and how to track them. I usually get a deer my first day. I just setup where I know they'll be."

Me: "That's amazing. Is there any particular age range of those that you've helped?"

Roger: "No sir. I've helped them all. Some women, too. But I won't go on a hunt alone with a woman. That would look a little weird."

Me: "Good idea. You live in Wisconsin, so how many deer licenses were issued last year?"

Roger: "A friend told me about six hundred thousand."

Me: "Really?"

Roger: "Yes sir. But only half of them got a deer."

Me: "No way! Why is that?"

Roger: "Mainly because they don't know where to go and if they *do* see one, they often miss the shot."

Me: "Very interesting. How do they feel when they miss out on a deer during deer season? Especially after missing the shot."

Roger: "Some of them don't mind, but most of them are a bit embarrassed. Especially when all the boys are having a beer at the end of the season party at Buck's Bar. Everyone who got a deer has a story. And those that didn't are all pretty quiet."

Me: "I see. How does it make you feel when you take somebody on a hunt, and you help them get a deer?"

Roger: "It's the best! It's kind of funny, but I feel better about getting them a deer than getting one for me."

Me: "Amazing. Do you think that there might be a few of those six hundred thousand that get a license that might just pay you to take them hunting so they could get one?"

Roger: "Hell yes. There's guides that do it all the time." I knew this all along; but Roger had to figure this out for himself. Then it would be real to him and not just my idea that he tried. He would own it.

Me: "Really? Do you know how much they charge?"

Roger: "I've been told they can make up to a thousand dollars a day."

Me: "That's interesting. How much did you make last year?"

Roger: "About thirty thousand dollars."

Me: "How much vacation time do you get each year?"

Roger: "Two weeks. I usually take it all during deer season."

Me: "OK. So, what you're telling me is that if you found nine hunters to give you $1,000 dollars each you could make $9,000 during deer season?"

Roger: "I guess I could." Then his face brightened up.

Do you see where this is going? Let's scale this business for him.

Roger can make an extra $9,000 during deer season that year. Then get a part-time business going on weekends instructing people how to shoot better. This way he doesn't have to wait until deer season to make some extra money. He could quit his second job in six months.

Those students become his next paid hunters and he raises his rates to $1,500 per day. He has more people that want help than he could service for the upcoming season, so he hires two of his buddies that are pretty good and split the fee with them. He makes another $1,500 per day from their efforts—$750 a day from each of them.

His shooting class becomes so big that he can't handle the load. He hires some folks who are even better than him at instructing and turns that over to them and they all split the profits. Those guys also quit their second jobs.

With the free time he has on the weekends, he starts making videos on tracking deer and puts them online. He gets thousands of subscribers. He no longer has to pay for any of his ammunition or equipment because the manufacturers give it all to him for free.

What's the moral of the story? When Roger focused all of his attention on making money, he was going broke and was depressed. Once he took his attention off himself and put it on helping others solve their problems, he became very happy and wealthy, all while doing something that he loved. The more problems he solves for his customers, the more money he makes. And has ton of fun!

This is a made-up story, but life's lessons are woven into it.

My hope is that this chapter has made you think. I hope you have been stimulated to think outside the box of barriers that you have created for yourself. We all have certain circumstances that limit our possibilities, but I've found that if I am always putting helping others first, there is a solution right in front of me that I have been missing all along.

Go back and answer those seven questions for yourself. I suggest you do it by yourself and be really honest about the answers. Others may try to "help" you by telling you how crazy your idea really is. I suggest you ignore them.

Obviously, putting a plan into action has a lot of moving parts. There is much more to growing a business than I can share in one chapter of one book, but the key is getting off to the right start with a clear statement of your Basic

Purpose. Otherwise, in my experience, all of your efforts are pretty much destined to fail.

This template may help you create your Basic Purpose (fill in the blanks):

My Basic Purpose is to help _____

who live in _____ by providing

_____ (your product or service)

so they can achieve_____.

This is critical to have a framework established now. Here's how this is going to work:

You create a Basic Purpose that is going to help a lot of people and one that excites you. Then we are going to create a Strategic Game Plan from which we will create Action Plans that lead to Results. The end product is that you will make more money to help more people.

My Philosophy:

It's all too simple!

If you need to bounce an idea off someone, I'd be happy to help. I have developed the ability to think outside the box. So, if you need a second opinion, my contact info is in the back of this book.

Hopefully, you have just gotten a new viewpoint for the possibilities in your life, but what you do next will determine if you make it a reality or have it end up just like Fantasyland at Disney World.

If you would like help in applying the concepts that I am writing about, you can get a free PDF of exercises I have created to help you get more out of reading "FUN AT WORK."

Simply go to www.funatworkthebook.com for the download.

It's all too simple.

Fun at Work

4

The Biggest Reason Behind Failure

Well done for making it this far in the book. Many will have disagreed with the message too much to get to this chapter. See, I told you that you were special.

My approach may have sounded like it will take too long, be too hard, or some other infinite number of excuses, but hopefully, at this point, you have an idea of what you would like to do to begin to help others. You have some ideas rattling around in your head and you can see some possibilities.

Don't be surprised if two things start to happen immediately: 1) you will begin having pessimistic ideas regarding how hard it's going to be, how it will take too long, or some other infinite number of excuses and 2) as you have these ideas and look at the impending barriers to your success, you will become afraid.

We can call this, human nature, or normal. We can say that we really need to be careful and responsible or that we need to consider the consequences of failure and we dare not risk it all. Do you think you're the first person in the history of the world to have to confront your fears and considerations in order to achieve something you consider worthwhile?

Let's check it out...

***

"The only thing we have to fear is fear itself."

Franklin Delano Roosevelt, Former President of the U.S.

"Your greatest fears are created by your imagination. Don't give in to them."

"A pessimist sees the difficulty in every opportunity; an optimist sees the opportunity in every difficulty."

Winston Churchill, Former Prime Minister of England

"Of all the liars in the world, sometimes the worst are our own fears."

"Fear defeats more people than any other one thing in the world."

Ralph Waldo Emerson, Author

"We are more often frightened than hurt; and we suffer more from imagination than from reality."

Seneca, Roman Philosopher and Statesman

"Fear is only as deep as the mind allows."

Japanese Proverb

"Everything you want is on the other side of fear."

Jack Canfield, Author and Motivational Speaker

"I learned that courage was not the absence of fear, but the triumph over it. The brave man is not he who does not feel afraid, but he who conquers that fear."

Nelson Mandela, former President of South Africa

***

If these quotes aren't enough to inspire you to conquer your fear, just google 'fear quotes' and you'll find some that will.

The point is that you WILL be afraid at some point. You MUST conquer that fear, or you will have NO control over your future circumstances.

My Philosophy:

The biggest reason behind failure is FEAR.

Many people advocate sitting down and planning out every step before they start anything because they are afraid to fail. They carefully calculate the obstacles and how those obstacles will be addressed. And they calculate and calculate and calculate and calculate……………… and NEVER START.

My solution is very simple:

My Philosophy:

START

My solution is get started. It's impossible to predict what the exact obstacles will be and the proper solution for them until you're in the middle of it. Then you hang onto your Basic Purpose for dear life and you'll figure it out.

My Philosophy:

Those who are afraid to start will never be my competition.

If I have seen someone else do it, and it's real to me that someone of my average abilities has done it, then I'm going to figure it out. And I'm going to start.

I'm never going to play in the NBA, the NFL, or the NHL. I wasn't born with that kind of talent, but if I wanted to, I could become a better basketball, football or hockey player. And I would become as good as I possibly could.

But I'm not interested in hiring someone to help me do that because it wouldn't help me help more people. You say "But, Dude, you have to have some fun and live a little!" Don't feel sorry for me. Remember that I never work. My work is my play.

And every now and then I "waste" a little time and experience more life.

I like Corvettes, and when I was in high school, I saw a 1969 Corvette Stingray, so I told my dad that I was going to have one of those someday. I've had eight different Corvettes since 1991. The current iteration is a 2015 Laguna Blue Stingray. It's my daily-driver, but I ordered a special performance package with special suspension and transmission so I could take it to the track and have fun.

There are companies that are run by professional race car drivers that teach people like me how to get around a race

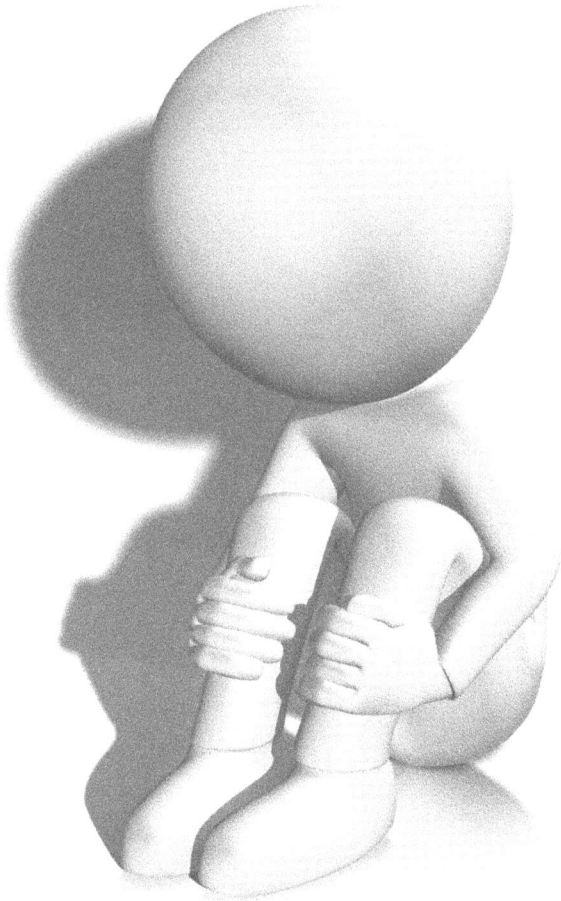

This Executive will *never* be my competition.

track, have a ton of fun, and not kill yourself or take your car home on the back of a wrecker. Lots of people have done it, so I knew I could do it too.

Am I ever going to race at the Daytona 500? Nope. But I've had a lot of fun doing something that many find too scary to try. And it really makes me feel alive. It really builds my confidence and teaches me that I can do more things that once scared me.

I've also found that if I am doing something that most others find scary then there isn't a lot of competition. The others are sitting on the sidelines thinking about it or trying to be safe. I'm out on the field playing. Sure, I get banged up and lose every now and then, but I learn something from that loss. I figure out how to do it better and get out on the field again.

I use the same approach in business, and I've learned a couple of very valuable lessons.

My Philosophy:

Losing in business is not going to kill me.

It might hurt my pride, cost me money, possibly bankrupt me, make me look stupid and incompetent, but I'm not going to lose my life. And because every game I play is driven by my Basic Purpose, I will learn something and come back and eventually win.

My Philosophy:

I usually have to lose before I win.
If you want to succeed, you will have to take some risks.

This attitude is what also led me to jump off an eight-hundred-foot cliff with a hang glider strapped to my back, buy an airplane before having ever flown a private plane, run ski trips for Indiana University before I knew how to ski, as well as drag my butt through dental school.

If someone has done it before, and they're willing to teach me, then I'm going to learn. Not try. Learn. Trying doesn't lead to an end result other than having tried in the first place. Learning how to do something and really doing it, gets a product of some kind.

I know that some have considered me reckless, irresponsible, crazy, insane, and weird. That has no effect on me because I am LIVING!

Travis Pastrana is an extreme sports professional. He has made his living racing dirt bikes and doing tricks while jumping that dirt bike. He has broken more bones than he can remember. He has raced rally cars up mountains where one mistake could cost him his life, and even jumped out of an airplane without a parachute—he had his buddy catch up with him, strap them together, and land safely.

I saw an interview with him, and the reporter asked him why he did so many things that were so dangerous where he could actually die. His answer blew me away.

"I've lived and experienced more than most people will ever experience in their entire life. And most people go through life trying not to die. I go through my life making sure that I live."

If you want to succeed, you will have to take some risks.

WOW! The interview is on YouTube with Graham Bensinger. If you want to be inspired, watch the whole thing. It keeps things in perspective about how he is not going to let fear conquer him.

I have no idea what Travis Pastrana's purpose in life is. I can't say that he is following along with what I'm recommending in this book, but he has obviously learned to conquer his fear in order to do what he is doing. And he is the best in the world.

I, personally, would never risk my life doing what he does, but what I *can* say is that I'm willing to risk my business life to help a lot of people. And I'm willing to put my financial life on the line to do it. Due to this, every day, every month, every year, I feel more alive. And I have a blast!

This is what I have figured out for myself and I have taught many others to do. You can do it too. You have things that you are extremely good at; much better than I am and a lot of others that you know.

My Philosophy:

All you need to do is figure out who you can help with your talents; then conquer your fears and START!

It takes courage. I've found the best way to conquer my fear is focus on my purpose more than the fear. To others I might look courageous. Actually, I'm usually a bit nervous when the stakes and the risks are high. I think that nervousness keeps me on my toes and focused.

When I'm flying down the backstretch at Sebring International Raceway at 140 MPH, heading into the big

Conquer your fears and START!

right-hand turn at the end, I'm nervous, but extremely focused. The instructor is in the passenger seat giving me instructions, so we don't both end up in the wall, and it sure as hell is exhilarating! And one hell of a confidence builder.

On the plus side, I can say that I've avoided a couple of accidents on the street because I knew what my car could do in certain situations and be safe. See, I became more capable by "living dangerously."

You hear about these wealthy, successful people all the time having gone bankrupt and coming back to succeed. And then there's the guy who went bankrupt and it ruined him for the rest of his life. What's the difference between these two people?

One decided to learn from it, reset his goals, take a different approach the next time, focus on the passionate goal, and start again. The other chose to be stuck in the past failure, be overwhelmed, and quit.

This may sound harsh, and it might be, but it's true. When met with failure, what will your decision be? Will you focus on your Basic Purpose, learn from it and charge forward, or will you embrace the loss and be happy with having tried?

The only thing that gets me going again after a loss is to refocus on my Basic Purpose. Who am I helping and why? What is the prize at the end? What did I intend to accomplish when I set out on this journey?

If I'm not excited about pushing through the stops and barriers, I have to refocus on my goal, purpose, and mission. I may have misestimated how hard this was going to be. I may not have had enough information when I decided to start this particular game. Now, I have to do one of two things; 1) recommit to the Basic Purpose, 2) quit because in the end the prize will not be worth the effort.

And no one can make that decision but me. Is the prize worth the effort?

I can ask others for advice. I can gather more data from those who have done it before. I can go off on the top of a mountain and consider my options or go for a walk; but in the end, I must make a decision. Same goes for you.

Am I saying that it's OK to quit? Hell yes, I am!! If the prize isn't worth the effort, then what am I playing the game for? To impress others? To not be labeled a quitter? Just to prove something to others? Trust me, it's not worth it.

Playing a game for any reason other than how it helps others is not worth it. I told you before, I really don't care what others think of me. I'm not trying to get others to like me or be impressed with me. I'm not taking all the effort to write this book to try and create those effects.

I'm writing this book to help you achieve your goals and live your life to the best degree possible.

So, how does this work?

After the decision to start, you will soon be faced with the decision of whether or not to continue. It's OK to decide not to continue, but then you had better *immediately* get busy on recommitting to the Basic Purpose; creating a new one for that game. If you don't, then that is quitting. It's quitting on yourself and quitting on the others that you could be helping.

If you don't charge on, then the loss can easily consume you. And the decision to not move on is made by no one but you.

What I'm talking about here is making a decision.

Pablo Escobar decided what to do with his life and so did Walt Disney. Hitler decided, and so did Steve Jobs.

I'm not going to turn this book into some philosophical debate about the root source of these decisions. Is Man basically good? Is Man basically bad? I'm not really qualified to weigh in on that. I'll leave that up to others, but I can tell you what I have observed.

We all make a lot of decisions every day. "Do I run the red light or stop?" "Do I eat that dessert or not?" "I really shouldn't have another drink, but what the hell!"

We've all made good decisions, and we've all made bad ones. What I have observed in myself and others, is that it feels really awesome to take credit for all of our good decisions.

When we make a good decision, we're proud. Some people want others to know about their good decisions, and to some it doesn't matter. But when we make a good decision, and everything works out great, we feel good about ourselves. And we gain a bit more confidence.

Unfortunately, when we make a bad decision, we start looking for excuses, reasons and logic as to why we did it or how it was someone else's fault. It's not much fun to say that we caused the bad stuff, so we deflect it.

Call it human nature, or whatever you want to call it, but it's just looking for a way out of having made a bad decision. The easiest thing to do is blame someone or something else.

That is death in the game of life and business because, once you do that, you have surrendered the possibility of you figuring it out and controlling your own destiny and future. If the problem is over there, then there is no solution, over here. Now you are a ship without a rudder, and you might just find yourself going over Niagara Falls.

I mentioned earlier that I met someone who is now a quadriplegic. He wasn't born that way. He had an accident and that was the result. I didn't know him before the accident, but I can tell you that what I observe right now is someone who is vibrant and alive. He is always looking for ways to help more people.

There was a moment after that accident when he had to make a decision. Do I accept my circumstances and charge forward with my life, or do I become a victim of my

circumstances and quit?

I could give many more examples, but I hope you have the idea by now.

I mentioned that I learned how to run my dental practice like a business and was semi-retired at thirty-eight. Well, it was a problem because I was actually a bit bored. I had won the game. I call it the Michael Jordan Syndrome. MJ is arguably one of the best, if not *the* best basketball player to have ever played the game. He and the Chicago Bulls won three NBA Championships in 1991, '92, and 93. He was named MVP of those Finals. Then he decided to do something that had never been done before. He retired to go play professional baseball.

Seriously?! Why would someone in the prime of their career quit to go do something they had never done before? I can only guess……………… boredom.

Hitting a baseball well is the hardest thing to do in professional sports. You're in the Hall of Fame if you get a hit three out of ten times during your career. The good players devote all of their energy to just hitting from the age of five. MJ hadn't done that. Instead, he had devoted his life to basketball.

He really worked at baseball, but after two seasons he returned to the Bulls in March of 1995.The team was in jeopardy of missing the playoffs, he was rusty and not in basketball shape, but they made the playoffs. They didn't

win the championship that season, but they won three more in '96, '97, and '98.

Why do I bring this up? Because it's a great example of what happens when you lose interest in your game and get bored.

I've seen some people get bored, and instead of finding a new game, they crash their current business. That creates the new game of salvaging that business. Nearly losing everything and then salvaging it is quite a game to play.

I experienced this to a degree when I got comfortable in my practice.

I was looking around the county for a second location. I had found a couple of possibilities, but it was interesting because I wasn't really all that excited about it. I really didn't know why.

The next event changed the course of my life.

I was taken to lunch and offered a partnership in the management company that helped me build my practice. I won't get into all the details, but in a three-hour conversation I agreed to sell everything and start at the company six weeks later.

That meant selling the practice, selling the house, taking the kids out of school mid-year, and moving to Chicago in January.

I had seen no profit and loss statements, and there would be no salary because I would be a partner. The partners either made money or didn't make any at all, based on how the company did. Also, my exact role in the company hadn't really been determined.

How could I make such a life-changing decision for myself and my family in such a short period of time? Easy, I would be helping more people by teaching other dentists how to build a better practice, just like I had already achieved. Rather than influencing a few thousand patients in my own practice, I could influence millions of patients by helping other dentists to grow theirs.

I can tell you my exact thought process before agreeing to do it. I knew they were going to offer the position to someone else if I said, "No thank you." I knew if the company was going to be successful and that it would be a regret for my entire life having to watch someone else succeed at the opportunity I had declined. And I really got excited about helping build a national company that would be helping thousands of dentists succeed and help more patients keep their teeth and live longer, healthier lives.

I sat back in a booth at a Greek restaurant in Chicago, took a deep breath and thought, *Winteregg, you don't have a hair on your ass if you say no, and you will live to regret this for the rest of your life if you watch someone else succeed at this.* That penalty was greater than any challenge from the barriers that I would have to overcome.

Also, for the record, for many other various reasons, it was also going to be better for my family to be in Chicago. This decision was *not* all about me. I'll save that story for another day.

Today, that management company is arguably the largest in North America, and therefore, probably the world. We have clients in forty-eight states and five provinces in Canada, we have a fifty-five thousand square foot building with seventy staff members where we train doctors and staff how to be effective and help more patients, and most importantly, we definitely impact millions of people.

That has been my game for the past twenty-five years, and I am continuing that game, but I've turned over some very key functions to competent replacements so I can expand my sphere of influence outside of dentistry.

And that is why I'm writing this book. To help you and many others.

OK. By this time, I hope you have decided who you can help by doing something that you love and are good at and are ready to start. How do you increase your chances of succeeding and minimize the failures? Read on.

If you would like help in applying the concepts that I am writing about, you can get a free PDF of exercises I have created to help you get more out of reading "FUN AT WORK."

Simply go to www.funatworkthebook.com for the download.

5

A Life Without Goals Isn't Much Fun

Now that you have a good grip on your Basic Purpose and you're willing to confront your dragons and go slay them, it's time to figure out some goals and plot out the Strategic Game Plan to achieve them.

In my experience, your goals can fit into three basic categories:

- Something you want to become - e.g. President of the United States.
- Something you want to be able to do - e.g. travel the world and not have to worry about time or money.
- Something you want to have - e.g. a new house with a Ferrari parked out front.

I can't emphasize enough how important it is for these to be *your* goals. These must be things that excite you and get you out of bed in the morning. It doesn't matter what anyone else thinks your goals should be. These are YOURS!

A job will become no fun very quickly, if you are doing it for someone else's goals and objectives. Maybe you are trying to make them happy by doing something you don't want to do. Or you aren't willing to tell them your real goals because it could end in an argument.

I can even live with secretly having your own goals that you don't share with anyone else. That's not the optimum situation, but it's better than having no goals at all or working for someone else's goals.

If you're the business owner, this is pretty easy. You sit down and write out what you want to become, do, and have over the next 3-6 months, one year, five years, and ten years. As I previously discussed, as soon as you start this exercise, all kinds of demons will usually come to mind as to why it won't happen; please ignore them.

Write them down. Start with a clean sheet of paper and no considerations. Whatever you want in each category.

If you work for someone else, it may be a bit more difficult because your goals may not totally align with the goals of your boss or owner, for example, you want their job and it's not available. If that is the case for someone working for me, then I want them to come tell me so we can talk about it.

For example: One of my best managers wants to own their own place. That's great! Let's talk. How about you help me figure out a new marketing strategy to boom this location and we can partner up on a second one in a nearby city? I'll help you achieve your goals, and you help me achieve mine.

I had a staff member once who wanted to become a paralegal. We talked about it, and I helped arrange her hours so she could get her classes done, then the transition for her leaving was very smooth and coordinated.

The other scenario would have been that she did it all covertly and one day gives me two-week's notice that she's leaving, and now it's a mad scramble to find a replacement and get them ready.

I always encourage my staff to give me creative ideas and help figure out how to expand their areas. If they aren't having fun at work, that really doesn't work for me. It's just a matter of time before they leave for greener pastures. If that happens, then I know that I didn't talk to them enough and never really got to know exactly what they wanted.

I'll get into this more later, but I think it's my job, as CEO, to make sure that everyone is aligned with the Basic Purpose and having fun at work. That means we have to talk about their purpose and goals. Then it's pretty simple to blend what everyone wants to achieve while really focusing on the Basic Purpose of the company.

***

"All who have accomplished great things have had a great aim, have fixed their gaze on a goal which was high, one which sometimes seemed impossible."

Orison Swett Marden, American Author 1848-1924

"Our goals can only be reached through a vehicle of a plan, in which we must fervently believe, and upon which we must vigorously act. There is no other route to success."

Pablo Picasso

"You have to set goals that are almost out of reach. If you set a goal that is attainable without much work or thought,

you are stuck with something below your true talent and potential."

Steve Garvey, Professional Baseball Player,

"By recording your dreams and goals on paper, you set in motion the process of becoming the person you most want to be. Put your future in good hands—your own."

Mark Victor, motivational speaker and author

"The trouble with not having a goal is that you can spend your life running up and down the field and never score."

Bill Copeland, poet, writer and historian.

"All successful people have a goal. No one can get anywhere unless he knows where he wants to go and what he wants to be or do."

Norman Vincent Peale, American minister and author

"Goals. There's no telling what you can do when you get inspired by them. There's no telling what you can do when you believe in them. And there's no telling what will happen when you act upon them."

Jim Rohn, American entrepreneur, author and motivational speaker.

"If you set goals and go after them with all the determination you can muster, your gifts will take you places that will amaze you."

Les Brown, American author and motivational speaker

"I think goals should never be easy, they should force you to work, even if they are uncomfortable at the time."

Michael Phelps, Olympic swimmer. Most decorated Olympian of all time with 28 medals.

"It's important to set your own goals and work hard to achieve them."

Yuichiro Miura, Japanese alpinist—known for being the oldest person to climb Mount Everest at age 70.

"It must be borne in mind that the tragedy of life doesn't lie in not reaching your goal. The tragedy lies in having no goals to reach."

Benjamin E. Mays, African American minister, educator and scholar.

***

So, do the exercise of writing down what you want to be, do, and have over the next few months and years. Pretend you're in Fantasy Land and have a magic wand. All you have to do is wave it and you achieve your goals.

Write them down now.

All of this comes with a very real warning label: If you really want all of these goals, and you want it to last and not be some flash in the pan,* you have to focus on how to help enough people to make it all happen—that's staff and customers/clients.

If the game becomes all about your goals at the expense of others, it will never last.

My Philosophy:

The more people I help, the more of my own goals I reach.

And the longer they will last.

If you would like help in applying the concepts that I am writing about, you can get a free PDF of exercises I have created to help you get more out of reading "FUN AT WORK."

Simply go to www.funatworkthebook.com for the download.

---

*Flash in the pan: Something that happened only once or for a short time and was not repeated

6

Create a Winning Game Plan

***

"Once you have established the goals you want and the price you're willing to pay, you can ignore the minor hurts, the opponent's pressure and the temporary failures."

Vince Lombardi, Successful NFL Coach

***

Sports make such great metaphors for life and especially for business. Teams have their own personalities, they have individuals with varying degrees of skills, they have to have a strategy to win the game and have to execute. Things rarely go as planned and teams have to be able to think on their feet and change the plan that they thought was going to win, in order to adapt to new problems.

Vince Lombardi is one of the most revered coaches to have ever coached the game. After all, the Super Bowl trophy is called the Lombardi Trophy. Oddly enough he didn't get his first head coaching job until he was forty-five, and he only coached for ten years. But we can easily say that he had a profound impact on the game.

To make my next points I've created a fictitious story of a movie producer from Hollywood, Norman, interviewing Coach Murphy after his Morningside Marlins just won the Super Bowl. Norman is curious as to whether or not this would make a good Hollywood movie and is gathering data.

Norman: "Today we are going to interview the coach of the Morningside Marlins who have just defeated the Dustville Dominators to win the Super Bowl and have taken home the Lombardi Trophy. They were huge underdogs and literally no one picked them to win. Their players were less experienced, and they didn't have anyone who made the All-Star team, in addition to having the smallest budget in football."

"So, Coach, how in the world were you able to upset the Dustville Dominators? Las Vegas had you at the longest odds ever for a Super Bowl opponent. All of the pundits* were bemoaning* the fact that you even made it into America's biggest game and how it was going to be a blowout; a game not even worth watching. So, tell us how you did it."

Coach: "Well Norman, I think that first of all, no matter what anyone had to say about us, we believed in ourselves. We had a team meeting, and we all agreed to not watch or read anything the commentators had to say about the game. We watched no television or read anything printed about us. We didn't read any comments on any social media outlet. We isolated ourselves from every source of bad news and just pulled together as a team."

Norman: "That's amazing. So, for the two weeks leading up to the game, you just had a, *no negative,* policy?"

*Pundit: a person who gives opinions in an authoritative manner usually through the mass media

*Bemoaning: to regard with displeasure, disapproval, or regret

Coach: "That's a great way to describe it."

How would Coach Lombardi say it?

***

"*Confidence is contagious. So is lack of confidence.*"

Vince Lombardi

"*Life's battles don't always go to the stronger or faster man. But sooner or later, the man who wins is the man who thinks he can.*"

Vince Lombardi

***

Back to the interview.

Norman: "OK, you had to come up with a game plan that you and the players could believe in that gave you a chance to win. Walk us through that process."

Coach: "Before leaving the locker room, after beating the Booneville Bravos to make it into the Big Game, I pulled all the coaches aside. I told them to go enjoy the victory for twenty-four hours. Then I wanted them to sit down and come up with a game plan based on how we could beat the Dominators with only the players they coached."

Special Teams Coach Smith had to come up with a game plan for special teams that, if his players executed it, could win the game. Defensive Coordinator Thompson had to come with a similar defensive strategy. Then the same for

Offensive Coordinator Jackson and the rest of the position coaches. Give me a game plan that could win us the game if their area performed to its potential."

Norman: "So you initially asked every coach to take responsibility for winning the game simply by looking at it from the viewpoint of, if their unit did its job, you win the Super Bowl?"

Coach: "Exactly. That's what we did the entire season. What I've found over the years is that if the offense is counting on the defense to win the game, and we lose, then there is dissension in the locker room. Players start blaming each other, fights break out, we complain to the media, and it rips the team apart. The game becomes a job that is no fun and a daily grind."

"The game then becomes attacking each other rather than figuring out how to beat next week's opponent."

"We had ten wins and six losses in the regular season. So that alone didn't make us undefeated; however, what I found is that every unit could look back at the game and see where they didn't execute and how they contributed to the loss. And as the season progressed, each coach and player took more responsibility for our successes and failures and became more confident because of that."

"At the first coaches' meeting after a win, each coach acknowledged what their unit did that worked and then what weaknesses were exposed that they needed to work on in the upcoming week of practice."

"At the first coaches' meeting after a loss, each coach had to review to the rest of the coaches where their strategy or execution failed. Maybe they overestimated the ability of one player or hadn't done enough research on the opposing players. Maybe they didn't predict how the opponent would attack their weaknesses and didn't properly prepare their players."

"By the time they came to that meeting, they had to have met with each of their players and gone over what they could have done better that would have led to a win; how, if that individual executed a play or particular assignment, we could have won."

"Each coach had to take responsibility for the loss and so did each player. Anyone who blamed another coach or player for a poor performance was fined $10,000."

"We did that all season. So, preparing for the Super Bowl was no reason to change the routine since that's what got us there."

Norman: "$10,000?! That's pretty harsh coach!!"

Coach: "We just won the Super Bowl."

Norman: "Good point."

Alright, let's break this down for a minute. We've all heard coaches say: "We win as a team and we lose as a team." It's very easy to look at a play at the *end* of a game where someone doesn't execute the way they could have and blame a particular player for a loss. However, we could also evaluate the game film and find plays earlier that, if others would have executed better, wouldn't have put the team in a position to lose.

A football team is broken down into groups. You have the Offense run by the Offensive Coordinator and the Defense run by the Defensive Coordinator. For the offense, you have the Offensive Line Coach, the Quarterbacks Coach etc., and the same breakdown of coaches by position for the defense.

A large team is made up of smaller groups, and there is someone who takes responsibility for each group. In business these are usually called Managers. A person that oversees several Managers is usually called an Executive or Vice President.

Oftentimes, there are employees that are designated as Group Leaders who report what is going on in their area. In my experience, if the group gets too large, it is easy for some employees to hide in the group and not pull their share of the load. So, five or ten in an area is probably about the right number.

***

"Individual commitment to a group effort, that is what makes a team work."

Vince Lombardi

"The achievements of an organization are the results of the combined effort of each individual."

Vince Lombardi

"A leader must identify himself with the group, must back up the group, even at the risk of displeasing superiors. He must believe that the group wants from him a sense of approval. If this feeling prevails, production, discipline, morale will be high, and in return, you can demand the cooperation to promote the goals of the community."

Vince Lombardi

***

From ideas like this I have come up with more of my philosophy on leading a group.

My Philosophy:

There has to be a plan to win the game and achieve our Basic Purpose.

Everyone has to take responsibility for executing it.

Therefore, you must have a strategic* game plan and there has to be a tactical* action plan that lays out specific steps that need to be taken to make the strategic plan work. You must take into account your available resources. How much money do you have? How many employees do you have and what are they good at? How can they be trained to do their jobs better?

A Strategic Game Plan that doesn't consider the available resources is a bad plan e.g. if your plan counts on

*Strategic: the overall campaign plan, which may involve complex operational patterns, activity, and decision-making that govern tactical execution.

*Tactical: of the actual means used to gain an objective

borrowing money but you have poor credit, then it is a bad plan. Get more creative and come up with other options.

It is critical that you take a look at every option and come up with the correct game plan based on what you have or can get. Just like a coach has to make a game plan based upon the players he has on the team. You can't game plan for an Aaron Rodgers or Tom Brady if you have a rookie quarterback just out of college.

A head coach who mis-utilizes his resources will not be a head coach for long.

A CEO who mis-utilizes the available resources will destroy a company.

My Philosophy:

Your Strategic Game Plan is determining the best way to accomplish your Basic Purpose while being smart about utilizing your available resources.

I suggest that the strategic planning be done by the executives and they then coordinate with the managers so that they can come up with the tactical action planning on how to execute it. Managers are closer to the action and understand what resources they have and what is possible.

It's very frustrating for a Manager to be given an action plan from an executive that doesn't know all the ins and outs of an area. They disagree with the plan from the beginning because it is unrealistic, and they can't get fully behind it. One of my most successful actions is to put people in charge, make sure they are trained to execute

Your Strategic Game plan is determining the best way to accomplish your Basic Purpose while being smart about utilizing your available resources.

their duties, and let them get on with it. I have an idea and then I run it past them to see if they think we can execute it. If they think a plan needs to be modified, I'm willing to change my mind, but I never take the pressure off achieving the objective and pushing forward the goals of the organization.

That's the owner/CEO role. Decide on the vision, purpose, and mission of the company. Then keep pressure on the group to hit the daily, weekly, monthly, and quarterly targets. After all, we have people that need our product and service and we are denying them our assistance if we aren't expanding, so we had better get going.

The owner/CEO makes final decisions that have significant consequences regarding forward progress towards the overall goal, i.e. promotion and marketing, strategic sales planning, filling executive positions within the company, etc. The owner/CEO also needs to make decisions on significant cash outlays* that affect company profits.

Another key point is that the resources you have are the resources you have. You have to figure out how to win with the resources available to you. A strategic plan that requires borrowing a lot of money, taking a lot of time to develop, like a new software program, or spending money to hire a new employee, will probably fail.

A good executive uses the available resources to push towards achieving the objective while making the area

---

*outlay: expenditure or monetary disbursement

productive enough to then buy the new piece of equipment or software and add to that expansion.

My Philosophy:

Make progress every day.

***

"Inches make champions."

Vince Lombardi

***

Each day move forward another step towards achieving the overall goal by executing the plan. You have to have some kind of daily battle plan. Many people do this. Simply put, there have to be steps that move you towards the overall goal and purpose every day.

This is more than a to-do list. Those items need to get done, but I'm talking about steps that need to be taken to execute your Strategic Game Plan every day.

For example:

Pick up dry cleaning is a to-do item.

Meet with Execs to be sure we are on track to achieve the First Quarter targets is a key item that has to be done.

It's easy to be very busy and, at the end of the day, not have moved the ball down the field at all. It's extremely easy to get distracted by other problems, requests, and demands.

Action Plan items need to get done and need to follow a specific timeline. If the task seems too difficult to get done, break it down into smaller, bite-sized steps.

I get involved in all kinds of projects and have many requests for my time. I help a lot of people and have very busy days. I can tell you from my own experience that, if I have a day when I don't do something that forwards my major goals, I don't feel good about that day when I go to bed.

Even if I only made one phone call or sent one email on a major program I'm working on, I made progress that day.

My advice is to take your strategic game plan and create a tactical Action Plan regarding what must be done to execute that game plan. Then you get the steps done, if it was assigned to you, or assign the tasks to one of your Managers or Executives. Be sure they understand the time deadlines.

If you're a Managr, get others to get the steps done. That's how you win.

The Action Plan adds up to a step-by-step program/project of daily activities that will execute the Strategic Game Plan. These steps are assigned to someone who will get them done and should include a deadline for completion. Each day, no matter what other life's emergencies and distractions hit your plate, make progress on one of those steps and you will feel better about your game and yourself.

My point here is:

Make progress every day.

You will eventually get there.

***

"Plan your work, work your plan."

Vince Lombardi

"It's not whether you get knocked down, it's whether you get back up."

Vince Lombardi

"Obstacles are what you see when you take your eyes off of the goal."

Vince Lombardi

"Don't succumb to excuses. Go back to the job of making the corrections and forming the habits that will make your goal possible."

Vince Lombardi

***

Now let's get back to our interview with Coach Murphy.

Norman: "Coach, midway through this season there were stories about a rift between right tackle Blankenship and right guard Jones. It seemed to cause a lot of dissension among the players and they started to take sides in the media. Blankenship was traded, and Jones was allowed to stay with the team. Can you comment on that?"

Coach: "For obvious reasons, I won't comment on specifics, but let me lay out the general idea. Our owner, Mr. Rich, knows that the overall purpose of the team is to bring entertainment to the community. He wants the Marlins to be involved in the community and help unite it. Naturally, we want to win football games, but we are more than a football team."

"I have to manage very talented and very competitive individuals; however, we all need to keep in mind our overall purpose."

"I personally spoke to each player separately with the Offensive Coordinator and the Offensive Line Coach. These meetings lasted a couple of hours each. In the end, let's just say that Jones was willing to recommit to playing Marlin football and everyone, including Blankenship, agreed it was best for him to move on."

"We traded him to the Rossville Ranchers, and he went on to have a great season for them. He's not a bad person, it just wasn't a good fit."

Ok, what's my point? The players in the game must be committed to the overall goal, purpose, and mission. Then they will be excited about coming to work every day. That commitment to purpose will get them through the hard times and challenges of the workaday world. They will be easier to manage and go the extra mile.

"A leader must identify himself with the group, must back up the group, even at the risk of displeasing superiors. He must believe that the group wants from him a sense of approval. If this feeling prevails, production, discipline, morale will be high, and in return, you can demand the cooperation to promote the goals of the community."

Vince Lombardi

"After the cheers have died down and the stadium is empty, after the headlines have been written and after you are back in the quiet of your room and the championship ring has been placed on the dresser and all the pomp and fanfare has faded, the enduring things that are left are the dedication to excellence, the dedication to victory, and the dedication to doing with our lives the very best we can to make the world a better place in which to live."

Vince Lombardi

***

Not everyone will have affinity for the overall purpose, or maybe even the product. When the going gets tough, it won't be worth it to them to push through the barriers. They should go find another employer with a purpose that aligns more with theirs. No one is wrong; it's just not a good fit.

My Philosophy:

Everyone, to some degree, must align with the overall purpose of the company.

Does that mean that everyone has to eat, sleep, drink, and breathe it? I don't think so. Naturally, I expect a higher level of commitment to my purpose from my executives and managers than those they manage, but everyone must believe in what we do in a way that is real to them.

In my experience, just doing something for the money can easily make the game no fun and not worth pushing through the barriers.

If *all* of us are committed to the purpose, we will be willing to push through the barriers to help more people.

***

"Every time a football player goes to ply* his trade he's got to play from the ground up — from the soles of his feet right up to his head. Every inch of him has to play. Some guys play with their heads. That's OK. You've got to be smart to be number one in any business. But more importantly, you've got to play with your heart, with every fiber of your body. If you're lucky enough to find a guy with a lot of head and a lot of heart, he's never going to come off the field second."

Vince Lombardi

*Ply: to practice or perform diligently

Create a Winning Game Plan

"Winning isn't everything, but wanting to win is."

Vince Lombardi

"Individual commitment to a group effort – that is what makes a team work, a company work, a society work, a civilization work."

Vince Lombardi

***

Here's a real example of that:

When my dental practice was rapidly growing, I had to hire someone to run it for me. It was becoming overwhelming to keep up with the administration of the practice and still be the main producer. I had two amazing front office staff members, but they were very involved with their families and weren't able to do the extensive management training that was required. This meant that I was going to have to go outside the existing team and hire someone.

I really wasn't looking forward to the hiring process - the ads, the interviews, the second interviews, the working interviews. No fun.

So, I cheated. I hired a patient who I already knew. I'm always looking for people with a great attitude that I can motivate to play a game with me.

Vince Lombardi has a great viewpoint about this.

"Coaches who can outline plays on a black board are a dime a dozen. The ones who win get inside their player and motivate."

One day, one of our favorite patients came in to have her teeth cleaned. We always looked forward to her coming in every six months because she was always in such a great mood and made us laugh. Let's call her Mary.

When I sat down to do her exam, I asked how she was doing. She said things were just OK. She worked in the accounting department at a factory and the local owners had just sold to a larger company and lots of things were changing. She was thinking about leaving. My ears perked up.

I called Mary that night with the purpose of explaining my expansion ideas and read her reactions.

I told her how my practice was expanding and that I was looking for an associate and an Office Manager. In a few minutes, I explained that my goal was to expand the practice, bring on an associate, get another location or two, and have her run the whole operation so we could get more dentistry out into the county and help more people.

To condense the logistics we went through, she agreed, and I paid her what she needed to make the transition. What sold me on her was her interest and excitement in playing my game with me and her willingness to try something new.

Also, she had questions about her pay and benefits, but because she was excited about the game, those items were easy to work out. She came on board for the game, not the benefits.

The point: your managers must be sold on the vision. As you're explaining it to them, watch the look on their face. Are they getting excited? Are they adding to your ideas? You can even ask them for their opinion on how to proceed.

When hiring someone new or considering a raise or benefits for an existing employee, it is easy to figure out if they are excited about your game. As an owner, you are looking for someone that can get excited about your Basic Purpose. That is truly priceless. Pay them a basic salary to play with you and give them bonuses as you achieve your objectives.

***

"Leaders aren't born, they are made. And they are made just like anything else, through hard work. And that's the price we'll have to pay to achieve that goal, or any goal."

Vince Lombardi

***

My Philosophy:

No drama.

What do I mean by that? It's very easy to slip into workplace drama. Complaining about one employee to other employees, complaining about a spouse or child problem, management complaining about labor, and labor complaining about management; workplace politics.

None of that leads to production. It just leads to more drama. I used to ignore it or think it was none of my business. They're doing a good job so why stir things up and possibly make things worse?

Well, over time I noticed that if I didn't stop the drama it always got worse. Sort of like a cancer. So now I handle drama at the first sign, the first whiff, the first cross look at me or another person. Something is going on so it should be addressed

Let me be clear. This is done not to make anyone wrong or call them out on the carpet in front of their peers. What if they are cross because their family pet ran away? Maybe they got some sad news about a relative or their spouse just lost their job.

Ask them if they're doing OK. Ask them if they disagree with something they are being asked to do. Poke around and find out what's happening. Help them.

People have lives outside the workplace and, if I can help them have a happier life, I'm going to stick my nose in and help when I can. Remember my policy of: *If you know me, you win.* That means, if you aren't winning, I'm going to find out why and see if I can help.

If you work for me, I'm going to make sure that you win. I'm going to respect you in the workplace. I won't take advantage of you. I will run the company, so you get paid and hopefully make a nice bonus. If your life is crazy away from work, I want to make your job an island of sanity.

All I ask of you is to do the best you can at performing the functions of your job, forward our company purpose, and NO DRAMA. I think that's fair.

***

"The price of success is hard work, dedication to the job at hand, and the determination that whether we win or lose, we have applied the best of ourselves to the task at hand."

Vince Lombardi

"In great attempts, it is glorious even to fail."

Vince Lombardi

"People who work together will win, whether it be against complex football defenses, or the problems of modern society."

Vince Lombardi

***

Back to Norman and Coach Murphy.

Norman: "It is very interesting that we have no footage of you yelling at a player. And many times, during intense parts of the game, we see your players laughing and joking around on the sidelines. We also hear of pizza parties in the locker room and team gatherings at your home."

"Many have interpreted this to mean that you're a soft coach and undisciplined. Would you like to comment on that?"

Coach: "My first response to my critics is that we just won a Super Bowl."

Norman: "Touché, Coach."

Coach: "Beyond that, I'll just tell you my philosophy about my job and what some people call work. My viewpoint is that if I can't have fun on my job, then I'm going to go do something else. Having fun doesn't mean being lackadaisical about whether I get the job done or not. It doesn't mean that I get to goof off."

"On the contrary. First, I'm going to be dedicated to the purpose of my boss. That's why I initially took the job. Then I'm going to figure out how to have a good time while getting the hard work done that's necessary to achieve that purpose."

"Second, I'm not going to enjoy my job by yelling at people and making sure that they don't enjoy theirs. I need to encourage them to continue doing what they're good at and I need to train them to do the things that they aren't so good at a little better. I need to give them responsibility for getting the job done and let them get on with it. I don't like micromanaging, so I assume they don't either. My main job is to be sure they are successful."

"And we are all going to have a good time."

"Let me tell you a quick story. While coaching in college at Tyler State University, I was blessed with two fantastic quarterbacks. They were both incredibly talented, but they couldn't have been more different.

"I'm not going to use any names here, but let's just say that quarterback A was very meticulous, precise, and demanding of himself. No one was harder on him after an interception than he was on himself. It killed him."

"Quarterback B was also a tremendous talent. My biggest worry with him was how to keep him on the team. He skipped classes, partied way too much, would skip his mandatory study halls and workouts. He seemed, quite frankly, to not give a damn. But could he ever throw a football?"

"During one particular game, quarterback A threw an interception on a guaranteed touchdown play. I was a different kind of coach back then, so when he came to the sideline, I was right in his face chewing him out with some not-very-complementary language. After all, he had just thrown away six points! He went over to the bench and hung his head."

"In the next series, he threw another interception. He came to the sidelines nearly in tears. Needless to say, my screaming didn't make him feel any better. He was an emotional mess, and I knew I was going to have to put in quarterback B. I was thinking that he couldn't do any worse."

"B started to bring us back from a twenty-point deficit. He led us to two touchdowns and heading into the fourth quarter we were down by six. Then he made a bone-headed throw that was intercepted. He came to the sideline and I was all over him. He absolutely didn't care."

"He looked at me, smiled and said. 'Call that play again and I'll get you six. I got this.' I wanted to yell at him some more, but I wasn't quite sure how to react to that."

"With one minute to go, I called the play again, he threw it for a touchdown, and we won. Coming off the field he came up to me and said: 'Coach. It's just a game. You need to have a little more fun and we might win a few more games.'"

"Those words haunted me all weekend. Maybe the kid was right. Maybe I needed to lighten up. So, on Monday, I threw

a pizza party for the whole team and a tradition was born. I never yelled at another player after that."

"I will admit that sometimes I raise my voice, but I've found that getting too serious and being mean to my players has not made them play any better. It often made them play worse."

"I decided to put the pressure down to perform and win, but to never take myself too seriously and to make sure that we always have fun."

Norman: "But doesn't that make you soft?"

Coach: "We just won the Super Bowl. I can't describe how much fun we had getting there and doing the hard work that it took. If someone wants to call me soft, I'm good with that."

My Philosophy:

Have fun.

***

"They call it coaching but it is teaching. You do not just tell them...you show them the reasons."

Vince Lombardi

"If you aren't fired up with enthusiasm, you'll be fired with enthusiasm."

Vince Lombardi

"Some of us will do our jobs well and some will not, but we will be judged by only one thing-the result."

Vince Lombardi

"Build for your team a feeling of oneness, of dependence on one another and of strength to be derived by unity."

Vince Lombardi

***

I have covered many key concepts in this chapter. I think the most important one is that you need to have a plan written down. Doing it all in your head usually won't work. It may seem a rather tedious exercise to do all this planning or even a waste of time, but life is so much easier when you are operating from a plan, utilizing all of your available resources, and controlling the activity that leads toward your main objective.

It's a lot less stressful and a lot more productive.

If you aren't the owner of the company, then do this in the area that you are responsible for. That advice comes with a warning, however. You just might find yourself getting a promotion with a lot more responsibility and a lot more work.

My advice is that you take the time right now to read the next chapter. It's a quick, short, and practical example of how to draw up a simple Strategic Game Plan and Action Plan for some activity. It follows an easy-to-follow pattern so that you can use it.

After the chapter, you'll be able to easily apply this to an area of your life or business that has been giving you trouble. It might take an hour or two for you to both read and write up your plans, but I'll bet you will suddenly see that it makes you feel so much better as what was out of control becomes under control.

***

"Unless a man believes in himself and makes a total commitment to his career and puts everything he has into it – his mind, his body, his heart – what's life worth to him?"

Vince Lombardi

"I firmly believe that any man's finest hour, the greatest fulfillment of all that he holds dear, is that moment when he has worked his heart out in a good cause and lies exhausted on the field of battle—victorious."

Vince Lombardi

***

PS: Norman, the producer, decided to make the movie about the Dustville Dominators' Super Bowl win. It was a blockbuster hit!

If you would like help in applying the concepts that I am writing about, you can get a free PDF of exercises I have created to help you get more out of reading "FUN AT WORK."

Simply go to www.funatworkthebook.com for the download.

Fun at Work

7

The Action Plan That Leads to Success

Hopefully you already have a pretty good idea of how you can apply Strategic Game Planning and Action Planning. My purpose in this chapter is to give you a short example and practical exercise to make sure that you can apply everything you learned in the last chapter.

***

"Inch by inch, life's a cinch. Yard by yard, life's hard."

John Bytheway (American author and educator)

***

There are a few key elements to keep in mind when creating your Action Plan:

- Each step must be able to be done in a reasonably short period time—ideally a day or two but not more than a week. If the task will take that long, then break it down into smaller steps. If the task is too daunting and intimidating, it can easily get skipped over and not done instead of tasks that are easier to do. The easier and quicker the step is to complete, the more likely it will get done.
- Each step must be assigned to a specific person for execution, and there must be someone holding that person accountable for getting the task completed. The CEO holds the managers/executives accountable, and they hold their juniors accountable.

- Each step must have a realistic due date. This is tricky. If the time given is too short, the person responsible could go into apathy and not start. If the time given is too long, they can easily put it off until the last minute—this leaves no margin for error, particularly if it isn't as easy as it looks. So, don't take this step lightly. There is a delicate balance between too much time and not enough time that could determine whether the task gets started and completed or not.

- Each step must be written down. Go over each step with the person it is assigned to and make sure they have no questions as to what is needed.

- Finally, there must be a method of tracking each task and making sure everything gets done properly and on time. People need to be managed and held accountable.

With these key points in mind, a reasonable Action Plan can be created and those in charge of each task can report when they have completed each step. Also, it can easily be monitored to see if they are on target and if necessary, give them some help to get each task done on time.

Now you should be able to see why it's so important that everyone in the organization is on board with the Basic Purpose of the company. Each of these tasks helps to push forward that purpose. These are not just good ideas or things we hope to accomplish. These targets need to be hit if we are to accomplish the reason for our existence—helping people solve their problems with our product or service.

Let's look at an example outside the realm of business that we can all relate to. Just remember from the last chapter:

There has to be a plan to win the game and everyone has to take responsibility for executing it.

We have all been on a vacation. Many are easy to plan but some are more complex. Let's use the Strategic Game Plan of taking a family vacation to create a Vacation Action Plan so you can get an idea of how this works.

Family Vacation Strategic Game Plan (Dad and/or Mom writes)

Take family on vacation August 9-15. Last year we went to the mountains, so this year we want to go to the beach. We went over budget last year and the next month was no fun trying to pay off the credit cards; so, this year we must stay within our budget. It must allow us to spend enough money on food and entertainment to enjoy ourselves without spending so much that it stresses us out about paying the bills when we get back. We need to have daily activities that will entertain the high school kids as well as the grade school kids. Mom and Dad get two nights out by themselves.

Develop a budget that will allow us to enjoy the location and activities of the area. Survey the family for beach locations that they would like. Find out what activities are in the areas and survey the family for daily entertainment they would enjoy. Decide on where to go based on location and desired activities, balanced with the restrictions of the budget. Mom makes sure everyone gets their tasks done by the targeted date.

Family Vacation Action Plan (Dad and/or Mom writes)

Available Resources:

A certain amount of money.

Mom and Dad

Teenage kids, Tom and Sarah, can help with the execution of the Action Plan.

World Wide Travel Mart (local travel agency)

Gail (Housekeeper)

Family Vacation Action Plan

_____Develop budget by May 1—Dad

_____Arrange with Gail to house-sit pets and plants immediately—Mom

_____Research beaches by May 15—Mom, World Wide Travel Mart

_____Decide on location by May 22—Dad and Mom

The Action Plan That Leads to Success

_____Research Hotels by May 29—Mom, Tom, World Wide Travel Mart

_____Research flights by May 29—Mom, Sarah, World Wide Travel Mart

_____Decide on Hotel by May 30—Dad and Mom

_____Decide on flights by May 30—Dad and Mom

_____Book Hotel by May 30—Mom, World Wide Travel Mart

_____Book flights by May 30—Mom, World Wide Travel Mart

_____Research activities by June 15—Tom and Sarah

_____Decide on activities by June 16—Dad and Mom

_____Book any activities that can be reserved before arrival by June 17—Mom and Tom

Fun at Work

_____Arrange for two nights out by July 15—Mom, World Wide Travel Mart

_____Check-in for flights on August 8—Sarah

_____Pack on August 8—Dad, Mom, Tom, and Sarah

_____Have a great time! —entire family

Let's evaluate this simple family vacation game plan.

Dad/CEO decides on the budget. He makes the money and has to be financially responsible. He's the one who was stressed out last year after he let the budget get out of control, so the budget is the budget, and the rest of the decisions pivot on it.

They could consider a five-star hotel instead of a four-star hotel, but then that would blow the budget. Mom coordinates with the travel agent to see if the plane tickets could be purchased any cheaper, or they figure out if driving would be worth it so that they could stay at a fancier hotel. Maybe a different location is chosen that's closer to home so there is no expense for flights which frees up money for a nicer hotel, five-star dinners, and more awesome day-trips.

Mom may want to create her own mini-Action Plan to arrange for two nights out with Dad. She needs to consult with the travel agent to see what is available, go online and check menus, coordinate with the kids' activities to choose which nights she and dad could go out, then make reservations etc. and has to stay within the budget, of course. That's a lot to do in your head.

If one step of the plan is too large, then break it down into easier to confront and more doable bites—each with its own due date. This makes it easier to have daily/weekly progress. Then the person assigned the tasks can feel like they are making progress and winning. This is critical to the execution of the Action Plan and the accomplishment of the Strategic Plan.

All of this is going on behind the scenes while Dad is out making the money to pay for the whole thing. He can get involved if he wants to; but I would prefer to let the people assigned their tasks just get on with it and make me a final proposal.

Everyone in the family feels great about the vacation. They have some say in what happens on the vacation and are included in the activity. They're happy that their skills were needed and utilized. Smart parents would also find a way to include the younger kids. This makes all the family members responsible for having a great vacation and everyone feels like they contributed.

Also notice, that after establishing the budget, all Dad has to do is decide. Mom is also included in making the decisions; but my point is Dad's work on the program was establishing the budget. That might have taken an hour. After that, he made the final decisions with his VP – Mom.

Those decisions took minutes because everyone knew what data they had to provide him with.

And this is how a smart executive gets tons of work done without doing it all himself.

If Dad gets into micro-managing this program with all the family members he is:

- Taking time away from making money or relaxing.

- Spoiling the game for the other family members assigned to their tasks.

- Basically, telling them that he doesn't trust them to do their task properly.

- Being annoying.

The CEO and the VP collaborate on writing the programs. They use available resources to write an Action Plan that assigns tasks to be done by certain people and those tasks are given due dates. The VP makes sure all the steps on the program are done by the assigned date and staff are allowed to go to the VP for guidance and assistance. There is usually no need to bother the CEO up until the time they are required to make their decisions.

The reason Dad decided to create the Family Vacation Game Plan this year was because there were parts of last year's vacation that were stressful and no fun. The reason they went over budget is that they didn't decide on where to go until the last minute. Then the airplane tickets were double the price of a month earlier—they waited to buy them because they hadn't fully decided on where to go.

They consequently paid more for their lodging, didn't get to do the activities they wanted to, and missed out on some restaurants that they wanted to go to. All of this combined to create some arguments among family members and ruined a couple of days of vacation.

Dad decided to act like a real CEO this year and lead the family on a well-planned and enjoyable vacation. There were some minor decisions that came up along the way for Mom and him, but the vacation came off as planned and actually under budget. They all had a blast! Dad even announced that the budgeted funds that weren't spent on the vacation were being diverted into the Christmas Fund, which made him a real hero.

***

"Plan your work, work your plan."

Vince Lombardi

***

Now let's take a look at how you can do this for your business. First, let's review the information from the Business Basics chapter:

Management

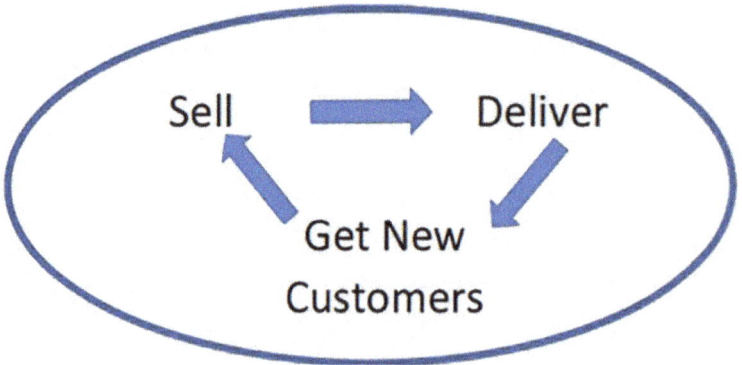

The Strategic Game Plan should take into account each of the four critical areas of the company. Evaluate them individually as to strengths and weaknesses along with the available resources in each area.

Here's a sample Strategic Game Plan:

- Main objective is to double our market share in the next three years.
- VP Sales to research a more effective sales training program to make the current sales reps more effective.
- We have had more quality control issues than usual. VP Production investigate current production process and correct what has changed.
- VP Marketing to research and present a strategy for expanding into the adjacent state to take on more market share.

- VP Administration to evaluate current scene in Human Resources as the quality of staff hired has declined in the past six months.

Now an Action Plan can be created for each of these areas following the above guidelines. Obviously, these will need to be monitored for effectiveness and modified as needed throughout the week, month, quarter, and year.

My Philosophy:

Someone must supervise the execution of the

Action Plan targets.

In my dental practice, it was my job to set the overall expansion strategy and objectives. I went over this with my Office Manager and made sure she was on board with it. We created the Strategic Game Plan together then announced it to the staff. This was done in a conference room away from distractions of the office. We showed the staff the statistics of what had been done in the last year and sold them on the vision for the next year—all the while never losing sight of our Basic Purpose to help patients have healthy teeth and gums so they would live longer.

Action Plans were created, and tasks were distributed among the staff with set due dates. These were recorded into a master log that the Office Manager reviewed regularly. At every weekly staff meeting, the staff reported progress on their assigned tasks. The Office Manager also let everyone know which tasks were scheduled to be done in the new week.

Supervisor

Someone must supervise the execution of the Action Plan targets.

The Action Plan That Leads to Success

The Office Manager and I met for an hour each week before the staff meeting.

Every eight weeks, we reviewed our progress in a four-hour meeting back at the conference room. Adjustments were made as needed so we could stay on track to achieve the objectives for the year.

Following this strategy, I was able to put my practice into the top 4% of all practices nationally in a community of only ten thousand people with eleven dentists—which, by the way, is double the number of dentists the American Dental Association recommends for a community of that size.

This system is very logical and methodical. I suggest you read this chapter, and the previous one, three times. Then you will really get it. Remember that executing your long-term plan, or really any plan with a handful of steps, is much, much easier when it is written down and not stuck in your head.

My advice is that you take the time right now to draw up a simple Strategic Game Plan and Action Plan for some activity following this pattern. Lay the steps out in the right sequence. Don't try to accomplish too much with one step but keep them bite-sized. Assign each step to a particular person and give them a due date for when it needs to be done. Then, check up on them to make sure they are hitting their targets.

Plan properly and you'll take out the stress of any major activity and spend more time producing and winning the game!

If you would like help in applying the concepts that I am writing about, you can get a free PDF of exercises I have created to help you get more out of reading "FUN AT WORK."

Simply go to www.funatworkthebook.com for the download.

8

Results Are the Only Thing That Matters

It takes a lot of hard work to sell, deliver, get more customers to sell and deliver to, then manage the entire operation to continue to repeat that process. But at the end of the day, there's only one thing that matters.

Did we do it or didn't we? No excuses. We either produced the result of the Basic Purpose or we didn't.

It may sound harsh but there isn't any room for excuses or reasons why we didn't get the job done. We were effective or we weren't.

We can sit around and make ourselves feel better by blaming all kinds of different circumstances beyond our control for our lack of results. But that doesn't lead to getting results!

It's simply wasting time being a victim and leads to no future results.

The economy took a nosedive in the summer of 2008 that lasted on into 2009 and 2010. There's no need to debate what caused it. We could sit down, have a beer, and whine about how messed up the politicians, banking, and Wall Street are but, at the end of the day, that doesn't lead to a company that is expanding.

We get world wars, recessions, depressions, bubbles, oil embargoes, stock market crashes, and terrorism. Not to mention layoffs, pay cuts, downsizing, and the boss's kid getting your promotion after you've been with the company for thirty years.

That stuff has happened in the past and it's going to happen again in the future. I guarantee it.

Here is the basic question you need to ask yourself when things go wrong. Really wrong. "What am I going to do about this? Am I going to whine, or am I going to figure it out and survive?"

Being a victim of your circumstances doesn't solve the problem. Have you noticed that sitting around and complaining about something doesn't make you feel better about it?

I've found, that the only thing that helps me, when things are going wrong, is to DO SOMETHING! Just sitting down, without blaming anyone or anything else, and looking at the situation starts to make me feel better.

Then I need to come up with a Strategic Game Plan and create an Action Plan based on my Basic Purpose and Start. Does any of this sound familiar? That's the only thing that makes me feel better and leads to surviving the situation.

By the fall of 2008, we had a real nasty situation at our dental practice management company. For almost twenty years we had gotten new doctors by sending out a direct mail piece promoting they come to St. Petersburg, Florida for a money-back-guarantee, $995 workshop on how to get more new patients.

All of a sudden, no one wanted to spend the money on the workshop or the flight to get to us. The old tried-and-true methods were no longer working. Statistics were crashing all around us.

The solution was for the executives to sit down and figure out a new strategy because the old one obviously wasn't going to lead to long-term survival.

The foundation of our new strategic plan was if they weren't willing to come to us then we were going to have to go to them.

In the past, I had a one-day seminar that I had done for some doctor study clubs on how to help the patient understand the value of doing what they needed rather than just what the insurance covered. In most businesses, that would be called selling. In dentistry it's referred to as, Case Acceptance.

We piloted our strategy in Miami, August 2008. We offered a free one-day Case Acceptance Workshop. We had no idea if anyone would show up for a free seminar on their day off, but we gave it a try. The result was that we got as many new clients in one day as we used to get in two weeks.

And it worked the same way the next month in Arlington, Virginia. The Action Plan evolved into me doing six of those seminars every month in major cities around the U.S., i.e. New York, Chicago, LA, Boston, Atlanta etc.

In 2009 and 2010, I was on the road for one-hundred twenty days each year. I treated it like a game and made it a lot of fun for the staff who were playing out the strategy.

Remember my philosophy of, "If it's not fun then I'm not doing it?" But it was a lot of damn work.

The result of that strategy pulled us out of our severely dangerous situation and eventually led to us *doubling the size of the company*. We took a potentially disastrous situation and figured out how to use that as motivation to expand the company.

That's what good Owners, CEOs, and Executives do. Because, if they don't, they go under and their competition, who is smarter and willing to work harder, gets their clients and customers. Swim with the sharks, baby! Survival of the fittest.

My Philosophy:

> **Blaming someone, or something, else *never* solves the problem.**
> **Focused action makes me feel better and leads to a result.**

Don't feel sorry for me about how hard I worked. I spent 2011 training my replacements and haven't done one of those meetings since March of 2012. The program has expanded from there.

The next factor that must be in place is having a way to monitor your results or lack thereof. It's critical to know if the company, division, or smaller group in the company is getting results. Looking at a P&L quarterly* is a very ineffective and lazy way to monitor your progress toward accomplishing the results of your Strategic Game Plan.

You have to monitor the production of an area with numbers of products or services produced. You can call them Key Performance Indicators, Metrics, Statistics or whatever makes you feel good; but the point is, you have to have a scoreboard to look at that lets you know if you're winning or losing.

My advice is that you immediately begin to monitor new clients, revenue, and some kind of production statistics right away on a weekly and monthly basis. You can get more sophisticated and measure other things like leads, closes, unhappy customers, promotions sent out, etc.; but the bottom line is, you need to have a way to monitor whether the company or an area of the company is being effective, or it isn't.

And I've found that the best thing to do is put the numbers on a graph so you can immediately see if a trend over weeks or months is expanding or contracting. There are simple software programs that can do this easily.

Deciding whether you're winning or losing based on opinion or emotion will generally lead to no expansion and no fun.

*P&L Quarterly (or statement): a financial statement that summarizes the revenues, costs, and expenses incurred during a specified period, usually a fiscal quarter or year.

Blaming someone, or something, else *never* solves a problem.

If we are after results, then doesn't it make sense that we have to have a way to monitor those results?

This comes with a warning label. Some around you are going to complain about keeping track of their production.

They will say that it's a waste of time having to gather up the numbers. Admittedly, it is your responsibility as an executive to be sure that you aren't making your staff do mindless administrative exercises to justify your existence, but I'm always suspicious of someone who doesn't want a record of their production.

Every job can have a number assigned to it so Management can monitor the production of the employee or area. What I've found, is that once you teach people to make a game of getting their production numbers up, their job becomes more fun and interesting for them. They usually get into the game of doing better each day, week, and month. And their results go up.

I get suspicious of someone who doesn't want to have their production monitored.

The truth is that in order to survive, a company needs effective managers and productive workers. If the managers aren't being effective, and the workers aren't being productive, then it will be reflected on the graph with a trend that is going down rather than up.

It's too simple.

Nonproductive managers and workers need to be replaced with productive managers and workers. I've found that my most productive workers end up making very effective managers over their area. I give them a raise and production bonuses as the production of their area increases.

This may sound harsh and unreasonable but it's the fastest, simplest and best method of achieving your Basic Purpose.

My Philosophy:

> **Monitor someone's production, and you will
> get more production.
> If you don't, then get someone who is more effective.**

As an executive over an area, it goes without saying that if the production of your area is down, you are going to inspect why it's that way and fix it. Staff may need more training to become more effective at their tasks. The area may need to be reorganized to become more effective.

It's a lazy executive who blames others for an area not being productive; who is constantly firing staff as the solution and constantly saying, "Good people are hard to find." No, they aren't. I have no problem finding good people because I'm a good executive with a strong Basic Purpose.

Do you know what many workers are saying? "A good boss is hard to find." My solution is to just be a good boss.

However, if the statistics of an employee aren't going up no matter what you do, then the solution is to find

Monitor someone's production and you will get more production.

If you don't, then get someone who is more effective.

someone else who can make the statistics in that area go up.

Interestingly enough, I learned this concept from my freshman football coach.

I was in a small country school and we only had fourteen players go out for the team—eleven are on the field at one time. The good thing about that, is everyone got to play. Our coach was very unreasonable and made us work our butts off in practice. I was definitely in the best shape of my life.

There was one event that I have never forgotten which has shaped my viewpoint of leadership.

We were playing a game and it had been raining all day. The field was a mess. To say that it was slippery would be an understatement.

I was playing cornerback on defense. It was my job to keep my man from catching a pass or to defend the edge of the defense on a running play. On one particular play, I fell down, and my man caught the ball. Unfortunately for me, I was on my face, right in front of Coach.

He was out on the field in a flash yelling at me. "Winteregg! That was your man!"

I said, "I know Coach but it's slippery out here."

He said, "You need to figure out how to stand up or I'm going to put someone else in who can!" I didn't fall down again. I had no intention of running wind sprints* until I threw up and then not get to play in the games.

What that taught me is, that as a leader, you need to get the people around you to take responsibility and figure it out for themselves. Or you need to find people who can.

That ended up being a very valuable lesson for me that I have never forgotten.

There's one last major point that I want to make before I close out this chapter. I've noticed that happy employees are more productive employees.

My Philosophy:

> **Playing bonus games will keep everyone focused on the prize.**
> **And make work a lot more fun!**

I need to have good working conditions plus fair pay and benefits; but having fun at work is a lot more than that.

It's my job to create more than just a good working environment. It's my job to keep everyone interested in our Basic Purpose and I believe we should all have fun while working very hard. Therefore, I always make sure that there are rewards and games in place.

For example, I always have a revenue bonus program that everyone shares in as the company does better. I've had

*Wind sprints: a sprint performed as a training exercise to develop breathing capacity especially during exertion; in sports this is commonly used as extra endurance conditioning or as punishment.

139

daily, weekly, monthly, quarterly, and annual bonus games. I've taken my staff to the Bahamas, along with their spouses, for four days. We've done shopping sprees to the mall. We had a quarterly game where everyone got to pick out jewelry from a local jeweler. And the reward for one game was we all got Blizzards from Dairy Queen.

The point here is that the reward doesn't have to cost a billion dollars; but there definitely needs to be a game that everyone can play.

It needs to be a game that forwards the Basic Purpose of the company. It needs to reward staff for helping customers solve their problems in a bigger, better, or faster manner. It needs to be for a prize that doesn't break the bank but is still something everyone can get excited about.

I generally consult my managers for advice on what the game and reward should be. They are closer to the action and know what reward everyone would play for.

Then the goal of the game needs to be a balance between not too easy and not too hard. It's a bit of a balancing act, but that's why I get feedback from my managers.

Then there has to be a way for the staff to know the score of the game and whether we are winning or losing.

For me this is a key point. Happy employees are more productive employees.

The bottom line is that results are what we are looking for. Statistics monitor results.

Playing bonus games will keep everyone focused on the prize.

And make work a lot more fun!

Effective CEOs, Managers, and Productive Employees can always solve problems and make the statistics go up. Then we achieve our Basic Purpose.

If you would like help in applying the concepts that I am writing about, you can get a free PDF of exercises I have created to help you get more out of reading "FUN AT WORK."

Simply go to www.funatworkthebook.com for the download.

9

Nothing Good Happens Without Profit

If I'm talking about business, there has to be a chapter on Profit. I know I'm taking a risk because there is a viewpoint out there that says profits are bad. Corporations are evil and care more about profits than people. Focusing on profits abuses the customers and the employees.

Granted, there are times when that is true; however, there are great companies that both the customers and the employees love. How would it affect the world if Coke went out of business? There are 1.9 billion Coke beverages sold per day in the world, so obviously the world *wants* and needs Coke to be profitable. Then the executives and employees can continue to serve people a product we love.

My Philosophy:

Basic Purpose must lead to profit.

Profit is the only way to stay in business over an extended period of time.

We can focus on percentage of growth or market share or revenue to make ourselves feel like we're winning the game, but if we aren't making more profit, why are we working so hard?

I know companies that are borrowing money constantly so that they can expand because they never have enough profits to pay for their expansion out of cash flow. That's one way to dominate an industry but, at some point, all of that debt needs to be paid back.

I'm not one of those, anti-debt, pay-for-everything-with-cash, guys. Sometimes it's necessary to borrow in order to expand and service the customer better. I'm sure the "no debt" guys have had a mortgage at some point in their lives, so they didn't have to live in a tent while they made enough money to pay for a house in cash. Although, there might be about 6% of the population that hasn't done that (you'll see where that number comes from shortly).

Again, this is a risky chapter to write. It's a tightwire walk across Niagara Falls. If I extol* profits for Management over taking care of Labor and the Public,* or if I extol taking care of Labor and the Public over profits for Management, I go over the Falls and I'm dead to you.

But isn't that tightwire walk what every business owner has to confront every day? How do we make a profit and keep everyone happy? If it's not done properly, the business goes over the Falls and a lot of people lose.

Naturally the owners, and possibly stockholders, lose. But what about all the employees that now have to find new jobs? What about the customers that were being helped by that product and service? What about all the other vendors that supplied the company raw materials and services to stay open?

*Extol: to praise highly: GLORIFY

*Public: a group of people having common interests or characteristics, specifically: the group at which a particular activity or enterprise aims.

When a business closes, there are many losers.

However, that opens the door for others to win. All of those customers are available to go to other companies who are still providing similar products and services. All of the employees are now available to be hired by companies that have better executives. The executives are available to now go find better jobs with a company that is surviving better in the workplace.

The bottom line is that business is a tightwire walk across Niagara Falls.

My Philosophy:

> **It's best for everyone for a business to make a significant profit.**

It's a balancing act with very little margin for error. It's nature's law of survival of the fittest applied to business. Those who don't do it right go under, and those that know what they're doing thrive. You have to be ready for that tightwire walk every day.

It's a jungle out there in the business world. Once you go into business, you are swimming with the sharks. There's blood in the water and your competition is just as hungry as you are and are quite possibly saying prayers at night that you fail.

So then, what is profit and what do you do with it?

Profit is money; and just like I said in the first chapter, money is not inherently good or bad. What people do with money is good or bad.

Profits are not inherently good or bad. What executives and owners do with profit determines if it's good or bad.

Profits can be used for unnecessary corporate jets or outrageous bonuses and lavish* parties for the executives. Or profits can be used to reward the executives and employees for a job well done; then putting the remaining funds back into the business so it can expand and service more customers.

One way for Management to approach a business/job is with an attitude of "What's in this for me?" They are trying to figure out how to get as much work out of Labor for as little pay as possible. This leads to large quarterly bonuses while the employees suffer.

We've all heard about the executives that got large bonuses after the company laid off hundreds of employees. That's not right.

However, Labor is also trying to figure out how to get as much pay as possible out of Management for as little work as possible. This leads to higher labor costs and makes it hard for the executives to compete in the marketplace.

As an example, I once had a patient tell me that he and his buddy had it figured out that they could sleep during half

*Lavish: marked by excess or abundance

of their shift in the warehouse because they covered for each other. That's not right either.

One manager even let an employee sleep at their desk for hundreds of hours in a period of four years. Really?

The "what's in it for me" attitude leads to dissention in the company with disgruntled executives and disgruntled employees. This leads to strikes that affect not only everyone at that company, but all the vendors and subsidiaries* that count on that company producing their products every day.

The best CEOs realize that Management needs Labor and Labor needs Management. This is the best example ever of a symbiotic* relationship. Neither side survives without the other; and that tightwire must be walked to balance everything out and keep the company alive.

A professional football team is a great example of this. Every player has their role. The center snaps the ball, the line blocks, the quarterback hands the ball off or throws it. Touchdown!

You can take the best quarterback in the league and he would get dominated if he were to play center. The center would make an atrocious quarterback. Each player has their role and each player needs all the other players.

The better they play, the more they get paid when it's time to renegotiate their contracts. However, if they aren't

*Subsidiaries: companies wholly controlled by another

*Symbiotic: characterized by or being a close, cooperative, or interdependent relationship

playing well, or get in trouble off the field, they get fired. Maybe another team will pick them up, or maybe their football career is over.

Therefore, a smart CEO will breed teamwork between Management and Labor.

People don't work hard for money. They work hard for purpose, a cause they believe in, pride in a job well done,

and survival for themselves and their family. They will do something for purpose and pride and be willing to not get paid; and conversely, they will do something they hate in order to survive.

But I will tell you this, an employee who hates what they're doing won't be doing it for very long. It's Management's job to create a good working environment for Labor. And its Labor's job to work hard so the company survives.

***

"Success is no accident. It is hard work, perseverance, learning, studying, sacrifice and most of all, love of what you are doing or learning to do."

Pele, world famous Brazilian soccer player

"A dream doesn't become reality through magic; it takes sweat, determination and hard work."

Colin Powell, retired four-star general of the U.S. Army

"There is no substitute for hard work."

Thomas A. Edison, American inventor and businessman

***

I once heard someone say that getting people to work hard is easy. Just pay them more money and they will be more loyal and work harder. I would bet a thousand dollars they had never owned a business.

I once had a great dental assistant leave me for a 25 cent raise while the office was closed, and we were on vacation. So much for loyalty.

Believe me, I've done this right and I've done this wrong. What I've found works best is to pay the staff a fair wage for a good day's work, then set up great bonus plans where they can really win when the company wins. When the company does better, they do better.

Sales reps need to be paid on commission. The ones that can sell survive, and the ones that can't move on.

This sounds harsh, but the business world is harsh. It's no place for softies. The good CEO builds a team of dedicated executives and employees, so the company survives every day while swimming with the sharks.

I have a white board in the Treasury area where everyone can see how much money we have made for the week and the rules of the bonus game are posted beside the board. At any time, any employee can walk in and see if we are winning the game or losing.

Who's willing to play a game when they don't know what the score is? We wouldn't *have* a Super Bowl without a scoreboard! So, tell the employees what the rules of the game are, show them the scoreboard, and let them go play.

When I win, they win. When I lose, they get paid their base pay and I may not get paid that week. In that case, I had better figure out what's going on and fix it so I can get paid the next week. The good execs eat, and the poor execs go over the Falls.

Do you see how owning a business is a tightwire walk?

My successful formula has always been to figure out a way to get the employees to take ownership for the financial performance of the company. When I win, they win. Then I don't have to run around the company motivating my staff. They motivate themselves.

This doesn't mean that we don't need Managers to troubleshoot an area and push production. What it does mean is that everyone's purpose is for the company to succeed and make sure the customer is taken care of.

***

"No enterprise can exist for itself alone. It ministers to some great need, it performs some great service, not for itself, but for others; or failing therein, it ceases to be profitable and ceases to exist."

Calvin Coolidge, former President of the U.S.

***

Nothing Good Happens Without Profit

It is Labor's job to work hard. It is Management's job to keep people working hard. It is the CEO's job to make the purpose of the company worth it. If everyone works hard at doing their job, the company will help a lot of people, be profitable, grow, employ a lot more people to work hard, dominate their industry, and survive into the future.

It will survive in good times and bad.

Anyone can make a profit when the economy is thriving. The competent are separated from the incompetent when the going gets tough. That's when your purpose is challenged. Everyone in the company is asking themselves "Is this really worth it?"

That's when the CEO needs to remind everyone the reason why the company exists and who they are serving—the customer. That's when the CEO figures out where things went wrong, fixes things, and fans the fire of the purpose of the company to rally Management and Labor to push through adversity and win.

***

"All the adversity I've had in my life, all my troubles and obstacles, have strengthened me... You may not realize it when it happens, but a kick in the teeth may be the best thing in the world for you."

Walt Disney

***

151

My Philosophy:

The CEO, Management and Labor must use Basic Purpose as the guiding light to Profits.

In my experience, someone just working for a paycheck is going to wilt when the going gets tough. But, when everyone is dedicated to the overall Basic Purpose of the company, the company survives. It becomes stronger, smarter and more capable.

This leads to the discussion about what you charge for your product or services.

The challenge in any business is to make it distinctly different from its competition. That differentiation can come in many forms, e.g., cheaper, faster, stronger, longer lasting, higher quality, better customer service, etc.

In my experience, way too much emphasis is placed on the price of the product or service in an effort to make the company competitive in the marketplace. There's this misconception that nobody wants to pay more for things, or everybody wants a deal, or we must be cheaper than our competition or we can't stay open.

Granted, there are certain industries where price is the driving factor, but I believe service trumps price most any day. People will pay a quality price for a quality product and quality service. Otherwise, how would the Ritz Carlton, Starbucks, Macy's, Mont Blanc, Porsche, etc. be able to stay in business? Especially during a recession.

It's all about **value**. How valuable is the product or service? What is it doing for the customer? The more it does, and the better it does it, the more people are willing to pay for it.

A motel with scratchy sheets and towels you can see through isn't much of a value; but while I was in college during spring break, it was cheap and perfect.

How do these kinds of establishments make a profit? They trim costs at every possible corner. There is no room for waste in any category on the Profit and Loss statement. All the executives, and all the employees, are about, "How do we spend less on_____," and that's how they make themselves different from their competitors in that price range.

My wife and I once stayed at the Waldorf Astoria in Manhattan. The basic room was $795 for one night. We walked into the room and there were fresh flowers on the table, chocolates, a small cheese plate and wine, the counter in the bathroom looked like a mini drug store with toothbrushes, toothpaste, mouthwash, special makeup removers, etc. The most comfortable robes you could imagine were placed in the closet with matching slippers. There was even a pant steamer and a shoeshine machine.

My wife couldn't contain her excitement and exclaimed, "Look at all this stuff!"

I said, "For $795 I better get some of this crap!"

It was a great value. I wanted to take my wife to Manhattan and have a nice weekend, so we took in two shows and ate at nice restaurants. Those were the fruits of our labor, and all those extras at the Waldorf made it that much more special.

The executives and employees at the Waldorf are about, "How do we make our guests feel special?" And that's how they distinguish themselves from their competitors in that price range.

The cheapest motel in town is not a competitor for the Waldorf. Nor is the Waldorf a competitor of theirs. The executives of each company know who their target market is, and they have to compete with other players in that market.

The fastest way to go broke is to provide Waldorf quality services for Motel 6 prices. I believe it's very hard to compete on price and quality at the same time and stay in business.

My philosophy is that competing in the higher-priced market is much easier than trying to be the cheapest in town. It's actually simpler because you have more money to provide better service and benefits than your competitors.

It's also a lot more fun to think up ways to take better care of the customer than to sit around and brainstorm how to cut expenses and save money. That's just painful.

Money allows you to provide more service of a higher quality than your competition. So, while your competition (in your price range) is trying to save money and make a profit, you simply charge more than they do and impress the customer with your product or service.

My Philosophy:

Good Executives *must* maintain the delicate balance between Top-Notch Customer Service and Profit.

If a customer ever complains about the price, just tell them why you charge more. *That's* your opportunity to make yourself different than your competition.

Guess what. This is another tightwire walk across Niagara Falls. Burn this into your mind………… never, never, never, never, (for infinity) criticize your competition.

When someone criticizes me, I simply see it as a desperate attempt to elevate themselves above me because they have nothing different and better to offer the customer. As a matter of fact, it's probably an admission that they know they can't match me.

And the customers don't like it. It makes you look desperate and unprofessional.

Think about it. Are you really that impressed when a sales rep or employee goes on a rant about how awful the competition is? I think it makes them appear desperate. I don't think it has any positive value, and you run the risk of looking like a critical jerk.

I once had a car salesman complain about the sales reps at another dealership lying to a customer. I knew at that moment that I was going to go somewhere else; then a few minutes later I caught him in a lie.

My rule is always take the high road. I generally say, "I'm not sure exactly how _____ does _____ but

Good Executives *must* maintain the delicate balance between Top-Notch Customer Service and Profit

I can tell you that I only use the best materials from the most well-known manufacturers, and I will stack my quality and results up against anyone." Or some version of that.

Rather than criticize, use it as an opportunity to break into a commercial about what separates you from the competition without ever saying a single word of criticism about them.

Charge a price/fee that allows you to drench the customer with quality and service. The profit is just around the corner.

My Philosophy:

Never criticize the competition.
Be better than them.

What I have personally experienced is that, when I know I'm at the top end of the price structure in my industry, it puts pressure on me to deliver the absolute best to the customer. There's money for replacing defective products at no charge and money to use better materials.

All of this with the goal of making ourselves different from our competition.

There's money to hire the best staff in the industry. They often leave a competitor who is trying to save money by cutting their pay. I hire them after the competition has them all trained up. It sure was awfully nice of them to do that for me!

There's money to give the customer the "Waldorf Astoria" experience. And they love it! It is so rare. While your competitors are trying to save money racing to the bottom of the ocean to compete on price, you've got cash to out-service them.

This isn't a new concept. Have you ever heard of the Baker's Dozen? It's the simple concept used in a bakery that when someone buys a dozen donuts, they get a free one. Thirteen instead of twelve. It doesn't sound like a big deal; but when the customer perceives two establishments to be the same, they will choose the one where they perceive they get a little bit more, especially during economic hard times. Where do they get the best value for their hard-earned dollars? That's where they choose to go.

To be clear, this is *not* an absolute. There will always be customers that want to get the best deal in town. They will spend $30 in gas and three Saturdays driving around town to save $20. They aren't going to like me, so I'm fine if they end up buying something of a lesser value from my competitor. There will always be that niche market.

I want to be at the other end of the scale. If they are paying for the best, then I put pressure on my team to deliver the best. We take pride in knowing that we *are* the best, and it really builds a swagger among the group that can't be bought with higher salaries.

Concurrently, I give my managers a profit bonus. While pushing up production, it's very easy to waste money on shiny objects and toys that don't contribute to the profit. I reward the managers with quarterly Profit Bonuses based on an increase in profit.

I'm not the only one, then, who is keeping an eye on being frugal with the checkbook. Wasteful spending that doesn't contribute to an increase in revenue is disapproved by my managers because it cuts into their profit bonus.

Recently, I did an interesting experiment. I wanted to know what the general population thought about the sales process, so I sent a professional out to Clearwater Beach, FL on a Saturday afternoon to get me one hundred surveys on how people felt about being sold.

I chose Clearwater Beach because it is a melting pot* of society. Some people ride the trolley and some park their car in the $40 lot across the street from the beach.

There were eleven questions total, but I want to share one of the results that stuck out.

The question was, "With regards to the sales process and experience, what do you consider is infinitely valuable?" In other words, what was most important to them when buying something?

Are you ready for this?

- 39% said they wanted a sales rep that was friendly, kind, and helpful.
- 19% said product knowledge was most important.

*Melting Pot: a place where a variety of races, cultures, or individuals assimilate into a cohesive whole

- And only a mere 6% said getting the best deal was most important.

Is that not shocking? People are three to six times more interested in being helped than they are in getting a good deal. Stunning!

You could say that I need to get more data for this to be conclusive and I won't argue with that, but I recently had something interesting happen that played right into this.

I had one of my business expansion clients look back at a log of customer service complaints and tally how many complained about the price. It was 5.86%. Close enough to 6% for me to count it.

Wait a minute! Does that mean that we are freaking out about our prices/fees being too high when, in fact, only 6% of the population cares? Pretty much.

And that 6% could care less whether you're in business or not. If you go under because you couldn't make a profit, they simply move on to the next business that is trying to be the cheapest in town.

My Philosophy:

**The customer that has to have the best deal in town
can go to my competitor and help *him*
go broke instead of *me.***

I prefer to hang out in the rarified air* of the higher end of the price range where I can deliver customer service, second-to-none, and the competition is minimal. That's how I make myself different from my competition.

***

"If you make a sale, you can make a living. If you make an investment of time and good service in a customer, you can make a fortune."

Jim Rohn, Author and Motivational Speaker

"Quality in a service or product is not what you put into it. It is what the customer gets out of it."

Peter Drucker, author and management consultant

"A customer is the most important visitor on our premises; he is not dependent on us. We are dependent on him. His is not an interruption in our work. He is the purpose of it. He is not the outsider in our business. He is part of it. We are not doing him a favor by serving him. He is doing us a favor by giving us an opportunity to do so."

Mahatma Gandhi, Indian activist

***

I want you to consider raising your prices/fees. It would be normal for you to be afraid to do that. You're pretty

*Rarified Air: Belonging to or reserved for a small select group; exclusive

certain that you would lose all of your customers and go broke, but you might be surprised.

I made a spreadsheet for my dental clients that revealed some very shocking results as to what would happen if they raised their fees a mere 10%. It meant an immediate average decrease of 6% in overhead expenses because the bills all stayed the same while the revenue went up. That meant that there was an average of 20%-25% increase in profits. It's simple math: revenue goes up; costs stay the same so that increase goes right to the bottom line.

I also calculated how many patients they could afford to lose if some of them got upset. Are you ready for this? The average scenario showed that the doctor could afford to lose 15%-25% of the entire patient base and still be more profitable than before the fee increase. And that would never happen.

If a doctor raised his fees by 10%, there might be a few families that leave the practice. Those would be part of that 6% looking for the best deal. The rest would stay because they love the doctor and the staff. The practice would now be able to provide better care and pay bonuses to the staff.

I also did another calculation to see how many extra patients the doctor would have to see if he *lowered* the fees to be more competitive.

This was shocking. If dentists lowered their fees by 10%, they would have to see *25%-30% more* patients to make the same profit as before lowering the fees. Unbelievable!

What's the point? What you charge makes a huge difference to your bottom line. I have a service where I can help you figure this out for your business. Send me an email.

The point of this chapter is to emphasize that as an executive, it is your responsibility to make a profit. Which would you rather have:

- A company with $2,000,000 in revenue and $100,000 in profit.

OR

- The company with $1,000,000 in revenue and $200,000 in profit.

My Philosophy:

Charge whatever you need to provide the customer with a product/service that makes you different from the competition while maintaining a profit.

If you can't sell it at that price, then fix your Sales Department. Don't lower your price to make up for a poor Sales Department.

Good luck with your walk across Niagara Falls.

If you would like help in applying the concepts that I am writing about, you can get a free PDF of exercises I have created to help you get more out of reading "FUN AT WORK."

Simply go to www.funatworkthebook.com for the download.

Fun at Work

10

How to Master Time

Getting results naturally leads into a discussion on Time. We have all used "no time" as an excuse for not having produced a particular result. That is usually not the case. What probably happened is that we inadvertently wasted a lot of time.

This is definitely *not* a chapter on how to create an effective To Do List every day and how to get those tasks done more efficiently. It is also not a chapter on the best day planner or app for your phone.

This chapter is about the three things that need to be mastered or you will become a slave to Time. Once you handle these, you won't believe how much time you have.

We have all said, at some point in time, "I just don't have enough time!" or "I need eight days in a week!" It can make life extremely stressful to not have enough time to fulfill all your obligations.

I have people tell me all the time they don't know how I get so much done in such a short period of time. I'm going to share with you how I handle all of my responsibilities and hopefully this will help you.

Indecision is an enemy of Time.

- "I need to think about it."
- "I'll get to it tomorrow."

- "This is a big decision…………….."
- "I shouldn't rush into things like this."

Everything above sounds logical and reasonable. But here is the trap—**eventually you have to make a decision.**

So, here's the catch:

How long does it take you to make a decision?

You ponder and think and discuss with friends and colleagues, day after day, and week after week, trying to decide. And you're doing nothing but wasting time!

We usually don't make decisions because we fear the consequences of making a bad decision. But what are the consequences of not deciding?

You just lost that great prospective employee because you had to think about it over the weekend; they took a job with someone who decided faster. You just lost that construction job because you couldn't decide on the final bid for your quote. I won't go on and on. You get the idea.

***

"I learned that courage was not the absence of fear, but the triumph over it, the brave man is not he who does not feel afraid, but he who conquers that fear."

Nelson Mandela

"Once you have established the goals you want and the price you're willing to pay, you can ignore the minor hurts, the opponent's pressure and the temporary failures."

Vince Lombardi

Not deciding is a decision to:

- Worry

- Think

- Be careful and safe

- Stop

- Not help (the most, deadly) your customers, your family and yourself.

My advice is to conquer fear and make a decision. Then get working on making it happen with all the time you would have spent, "thinking about it."

My Philosophy:

**Not making a decision is a decision to not decide...
and waste time.**

I covered the subject of fear earlier, but it bears repeating. Not only does fear take you out of the game, and make it no fun, but it also wastes a tremendous amount of time.

Whatever effort you put into that decision was a complete waste of time unless you do step two:

START!

I covered this earlier as well, but the point here is that you WILL be afraid at some point and you will hesitate to start to execute your decision. You MUST conquer fear, or you will have NO control over time.

Many people advocate sitting down and planning out every step before they start anything. They carefully calculate what the obstacles are and how those obstacles will be addressed. And they calculate, and calculate, and calculate, and calculate………………. and NEVER START.

Your time is much better spent throwing yourself into it and figuring it out as you go. Then, after you have decided *what* to do the next thing to do is:

START

Just get started. It's impossible to predict what the exact obstacles will be, and the proper solution for them, until you're in the middle of it.

If I have seen someone else do this thing, then therefore, someone of my abilities has done it. I know I can figure it out, and I'm going to start now.

I understand that it's scary, but we talked about that earlier. Overcome your fear and START. It's the only way you will ever accomplish something in life.

And it's the only way you will ever avoid wasting a ton of Time!

The impulse is to be safe and careful. But isn't that exactly what your competition is doing?

I consider that I don't have much competition. Why? Because I make a decision, I start, and I don't quit. If there's someone else in my field that does that then, "Let the games begin, baby!" That's competition in business.

"If everything seems under control, you're just not going fast enough."

Mario Andretti, Indianapolis 500 1969 Winner

***

What is the difference between a Hall of Fame NFL Quarterback and someone who can't get off the practice squad? The Hall of Famer can quickly analyze the defense, *decide* where to throw the ball, and **throw it**.

The practice squad QB may be able to do those things, but just not fast enough.

The key is to not just decide, but to ACT!

My Philosophy:

I'm going to make a decision and then I'm going to Start.

If my decision was wrong, I'll find out fast, adjust my plan and start the next idea.

Thinking about it is not acting on it and is a tremendous waste of time. I get a lot done in a very short period of time because I decide, and I act.

I have a planner that I use to help me get critical targets done each day. And each day I strive to push forward every project that I'm responsible for. But one thing I don't do is waste time.

Delegate

Finally, I've seen very many capable executives/business owners work themselves to death. They complain about how they are overworked and have no time. They don't take vacations because they are so swamped with project after project.

I don't have that problem for one very simple reason:

I delegate!

I'll bet you're a lot like me. I feel great when I've helped someone! They had a problem and I helped them solve it. That's why I get out of bed in the morning.

I have great news for you: your *best* employees **feel the same way**! They get out of bed in the morning to help others. Not everyone is like this, just the best ones.

My question to the overworked executive/business owner then is: "Why are you taking away all the fun of helping you from your employees?"

What I usually observe, is that the overworked executive has some great people who are very **willing to help** and **not being utilized just standing around** while the executive goes up in smoke.

This baffles me. Are they afraid the employees will mess up? Are they afraid they will cost the company money? Are they afraid they will lose some customers? I have news for you. Of course, they will! But all **this is already happening** while they stand around watching you burn yourself out. So why not turn over some of your simpler tasks to competent staff and **let them help you**?!

I'm going to let you in on one of my biggest secrets and successful actions as an executive: I'm always looking for my replacement. Then I train them to take over my responsibilities. I monitor their production with statistics and help them become more effective until they are a competent replacement for me.

Look for someone who is passionate about the company, someone you can apprentice for a few years, someone to gradually give more and more responsibility to, and someone you can be patient with. Like one of your kids, or an employee who has been with you for a long time.

Always be looking for good managers and productive workers. Throughout your day, notice how you are treated when you are the customer somewhere else. I have no problem hiring someone away from another business if they have treated me awesomely.

Groom your successor. Then work until you're a hundred. By the time you've been in business for ten or twenty years, or more, your greatest value will be all of your experience and connections. Stay active in the business but turn over the day-to-day challenges to your replacements.

Become a consultant to your own company. There are so many ways to participate and contribute without working sixty-hour weeks, but you have to **empower** and **reward** those around you as you grow the company.

And look at all the time you just created.

My Philosophy:

I'm always looking for my replacement.

This gives me lots of time to do other things.

You create time by deciding, then starting and getting others to help free you up.

In the end, it makes the job a lot more fun for you and those competent staff around you.

If you would like help in applying the concepts that I am writing about, you can get a free PDF of exercises I have created to help you get more out of reading "FUN AT WORK."

Simply go to www.funatworkthebook.com for the download.

You create time by deciding, then starting and getting others to help free you up.

Fun at Work

11

You Won't Achieve Much Without Communication

I want you to consider that how well you communicate, and how many people you communicate with, determines the size of your world. What does that mean?

Let's look at two examples:

1. A hermit lives by himself in the mountains. He has retreated from life and built a cabin with his own hands. He has a dog that keeps him company. He hunts and fishes for his own food, goes into a small town to get basic supplies once a month and talks to the store owner. His world is as big as his cabin, his dog, and the store owner.
2. The president of the United States can get anyone in the world on the phone and talk with them.

These are two extreme examples of how communication determines the size of your world.

Say you just had a fight with someone and don't want to talk to them because you're mad. They are no longer part of your world and your world got smaller.

You have someone that you share all of your deepest thoughts with. They are part of your world and your world is bigger because of that.

The boss that has staff meetings, lets the team know what is happening, and encourages them, is in better communication than the boss that just yells. Yelling can be a form of communication, but I prefer talking to people and asking them questions about how things are going and what they think should be done to handle a situation. Then they get to say something. That works better for me than yelling.

Consider that the person who returns phone calls and emails has a bigger world than the person who doesn't.

This chapter will probably be the shortest chapter but that has nothing to do with how important communication is.

We have covered the value of establishing who you are going to help and how you're going to do it with your Game Plan. We have talked about how to price your product/service to make a profit. The final step is pretty obvious:

My Philosophy:

The executives need to keep everyone informed of what is happening and where the company is going.

I've talked to business owners that grumble about how their employees aren't motivated or not working hard enough. Then I ask when they last held a meeting to let everyone know what was happening in the company. They said, "Never."

If I don't know the score in the game I'm playing, or why I'm playing it, then I'm not going to be motivated or work very hard either.

So, what good is a game plan if the coach never explains it to the team?!

The executives need to keep everyone informed of what is happening and where the company is going.

My advice is that the manager over each area has a daily meeting to go over what the plan is for the day. Discuss where the potential problems could arise, coordinate with the other members of the team, and make a plan for what each member of the unit is doing that day, etc. Also, give production quotas for the day and get with your team to go over what the objective is for being at work that day.

This way everyone knows what all the team members are doing and thinking.

There should be weekly staff meetings where everyone from different units gets together and looks over the past week. What was the score? Did we win last week, or did we lose? What's the plan for this week? What is the production quota for each area this week?

The CEO/owner needs to meet with the Managers weekly, monthly, quarterly and annually. Each meeting taking a broader look at the Strategic Game Plan and Action Plan to make sure that progress is being made. It would be normal that adjustments must be made based on the statistics that are being monitored.

Isn't this what happens during breaks of an athletic contest? Imagine a coach going up into a VIP suite during halftime and letting the players just figure it out for themselves. He would be fired the next day.

The point is, don't just go through all the work we have been covering so far and keep it to yourself. You will not have a company of any significant size without employees; and you will not win the game if you don't tell those employees what the Game Plan is.

Then everyone has fun and you all win. They will have contributed to that win and had a lot of fun doing it.

My Philosophy:

It's the job of the executives in the company to keep everyone informed of what is happening and where the company is going.

***

"The art of communication is the language of leadership."

James Hulse, Author

"The single biggest problem in communication is the illusion that it has taken place."

George Bernard Shaw, Author

"Collaboration is a key part of the success of any organization, executed through a clearly defined vision and mission and based on transparency and constant communication.

Dinesh Paliwal, Indian-American businessman

"Communication is a skill that you can learn. It's like riding a bicycle or typing. If you're willing to work at it, you can rapidly improve the quality of every part of your life."

Brian Tracy, Canadian-American motivational speaker and author

"It's about communication. It's about honesty. It's about treating people in the organization as deserving to know the facts. You don't try to give them half the story. You don't try to hide the story. You treat them as - as true equals, and you communicate, and you communicate, and communicate."

Louis V. Gerstner, Jr., Former CEO of IBM

***

Like all of the concepts I'm writing about, communication can be used to create, and it can be used to destroy. My advice is to always fall on the create side of the fence.

That means, when you are communicating, you need to take responsibility for how that communication will be received and how you are going to deliver it. Using a lot of force in your communication is necessary if you're telling others what to do when evacuating a burning house, but it's ineffective when trying to sing a lullaby to get a baby to go to sleep.

The point here is to not use a baseball bat when a nerf* bat will get the job done. Assess the situation and deliver the communication in such a way that will bring about an understanding and a desired positive result.

.

*Nerf: Nerf is a toy brand created by Parker Brothers and currently owned by Hasbro. Most of the toys are a variety of foam-based weaponry, with other Nerf products including balls for sports like American football, basketball and baseball

I personally think that yelling or being mean is rarely needed.

We've all made mistakes and said something that didn't come out right. We have all created upsets. The immediate reaction is to stop communicating, but that doesn't have much chance of resolving an upset.

If you mess up a communication, go back and fix it. The rule is keep talking, and that will work about 80% of the time. (What to do with the other 20% is in the next chapter)

***

"Words are singularly the most powerful force available to humanity. We can choose to use this force constructively with words of encouragement, or destructively using words of despair. Words have energy and power with the ability to help, to heal, to hinder, to hurt, to harm, to humiliate and to humble."

Yehuda Berg, author

***

Words are powerful. They can be used to create or destroy. You must communicate; but, do so wisely and make your world bigger every day. Believe me. Do this and have a lot more fun.

If you would like help in applying the concepts that I am writing about, you can get a free PDF of exercises I have created to help you get more out of reading "FUN AT WORK." Simply go to www.funatworkthebook.com for the download.

12

You Can't Help Them All

In every industry there are specialists. There are certain problems that require more knowledge, skill, and ability than the average human naturally possesses. On every athletic team, there are players who were born with natural talents and abilities that give them special skills. These specialists practice to improve their skills so they can have specialized roles in solving the problems of their chosen game.

In business, there are consultants that specialize in helping companies solve complex problems to help the company accomplish its mission and purpose. There are even independent contractors that go from company to company to solve very technical problems and that's how they make their living.

Have you ever noticed that some people specialize in creating problems?

There's a very optimistic saying that states, "There's a silver lining in every cloud." I like that viewpoint. When something is going wrong and making your day cloudy, this type of person will always be looking for ways to turn the lemons into lemonade. In other words, "These are our circumstances. How do we make this work?"

I love those people! Nothing seems to be going right. All hell is breaking loose. It's getting incredibly stressful. The situation has dire consequences if it's not figured out, the walls seem to be moving in and the stress is through the roof!

And someone steps up and says: "We are going to figure this out." "I have an idea... What about _____?"

There is a flicker of hope in your universe while they make you feel like you aren't all alone with no answers. It is no longer hopeless. You begin to get the idea that maybe there is at least *one* possible solution. You aren't out of the woods yet, but it at least seems like something can be done and all of a sudden things don't seem hopeless.

During times of crisis these individuals are worth their weight in gold. I'm going to call them, "Golden Gilda," and "Solution Sam."

There are also people who operate in the opposite manner. They seem to be able to find a black cloud on the most beautiful sunny day. No matter how good things are going, they bring up some way that all could be lost in the future. Profits have been up for three quarters in a row, yet they just provided you with several articles they found online that say how the economy is about to crash, or that your competition has just hired some hotshot CEO. Or even that your competitor is coming to town so this period of abundance could end at any minute. They specialize in creating problems.

All of a sudden, you don't feel as happy as you were a few minutes ago. You go to lunch but seem to have lost your appetite. Maybe you get a headache. Overall, life doesn't seem so good anymore, and the next day they do it again.

They specialize in finding the problem in every situation. Instead of living from the viewpoint of, "If this happens, here's what we can do about it," it's more like, "If this happens, we are doomed!"

Some of them are even better at this than others. They don't just find a black cloud on a sunny day, they find a tornado, moving fast and furiously to destroy everything. Even this group has its highly-trained specialists.

I'm going to call these people, "Debbie Downer," and "Problem Pete."

The part that becomes so confusing is that they usually say, "I'm just trying to help." They present their case with enough logic that it seems plausible that it actually could all go wrong, and all would be lost.

Golden Gilda and Solution Sam have the ability to look at a negative situation and see how it could go right. Debbie Downer and Problem Pete have the ability to look at a positive situation and see how it could go wrong.

As an owner/CEO/Executive, who would you like to surround yourself with?

Let me tell you a couple of my own personal experiences and observations that you might be able to relate to.

I graduated from dental school in 1981. Afterwards, I bought a small practice in a farm town in northern Indiana, and three employees decided to stay from the last doctor.

I was the new guy, and I was a bit nervous about taking over a practice from a retiring dentist that the patients loved. I invested everything I had, plus borrowed $50,000 at 19% to get the practice open. (Prime interest back then was at 21% and the banker, "helped me out," on the loan)

This was everything that I had spent eight years working for. So, on the one hand, I was excited but nervous on the other.

Regardless, I opened in July. One of the carried over staff members was, "just trying to help," by telling me how things worked in this little town. Who knew who, who was connected, and who to be careful with. She was just full of all kinds of "advice." She wasn't just a Debbie Downer, she turned out to be a real Sneaky Susan. (By the way, I never employed anyone named Susan. These names have been changed to protect the guilty.)

I was twenty-seven at the time. I was in pretty good health; but around that time, I started to get stomach cramps. I seemed to have no energy, and would come home from the office, have dinner, and fall asleep on the couch. Over Labor Day, I bent over to pick up the newspaper and my back went into a total spasm. Luckily, I had a patient who was a chiropractor and he met me at his office and helped me, but I had to see him every day that week just to be able to work.

Then, in October, I ended up in the emergency room with terrible stomach cramps. (The surgeon in town was also a patient of mine.) He did an exam on me and said, "I think I have a date with your appendix today." I remember the look on his face when he told me that all of my bloodwork came back normal because nothing felt normal to me.

It was quite troubling to be so young and have all this happening to my body.

Then something interesting happened. For personal reasons, Sneaky Susan took a four-month Leave of Absence.* I scrambled to find temporary help to replace her, which is always a bit annoying because a temp doesn't know the ins and outs of how things work, but we were getting through it.

After Susan had been gone for a few weeks, my wife asked me how my stomach was feeling. I had actually forgotten about it. My back was getting better, and I was now on a monthly maintenance program with my chiropractor instead of weekly.

That winter things were a bit slow, but I was paying the bills and having fun in my new profession. Then, I got notice that Sneaky Susan was ready to come back in two weeks. This would normally be a relief because things could get back to normal, but in my case, my stomach started to hurt again.

My wife and I were talking about it, and we realized that I got better after she left and worse at even the thought of her coming back. So, I knew right there that I had to confront not letting her back into the practice.

This was terrible. She had been in the practice for years. She knew all the patients and everybody in town. If I let her go, she could go to another office and take half the

*Leave of Absence: permission to be absent from duty or employment

187

practice with her. She could even bad-mouth me all over this small town.

I had to confront all of those consequences and decided that my health was more important than any employee or possible business risk. My wife was working as a nurse and was willing to put in more hours, and I could get an associate job in South Bend if the practice slowed down. We were willing to work our asses off to cover our bills and loan payments if we had to.

We decided that no matter the circumstances, Sneaky Susan couldn't come back into the practice. My wife is awesome!

The interesting thing is that, once we worked out our battle plan and were willing to confront the circumstances, I felt relief. My stomach quit hurting. I was nervous about telling Sneaky Susan she couldn't come back to the office, but I also had a particular calm about me because I had a solution as to what we would do if this turned out badly. That gave me a bit of confidence.

I can't describe how uncomfortable it was to tell Sneaky Susan that she couldn't come back to the practice. She got very upset and assured me that this was a big mistake. She even went as far as telling the doctor I had purchased the practice from, and he came to the office and yelled at me, assuring me that this was my doom.

It's very interesting that my stomach didn't hurt at all during this time of turmoil. I was actually quite calm.

Another interesting development was that there were ten other dentists in town, but no one hired her.

Luckily, no disaster ever happened. Over that next summer, my practice continued to grow, and life was great. A year later we bought our first house and started our family soon thereafter. My wife never had to work extra hours, and the practice was doing just fine.

So, here's my advice: Debbie Downer and Problem Pete don't bring enough to the game to make the advantages of keeping them better than the consequences of letting them go.

I hated firing staff; but if you are going to take responsibility for the well-being of the group, there are times when it just needs to be done. I think it's the worst part of owning your own business but making the tough decisions to do what's best for the group is what separates those who succeed from those who fail. It separates those who just get by from those who flourish.

I will admit there may have been times when I let someone go that could have been salvaged. I'm far from perfect, and can take responsibility for my errors; but I would rather fire someone I maybe shouldn't have, than to be reasonable and keep a Problem Pete in the group.

Remember, it's a tightwire walk across Niagara Falls and it's most definitely swimming with the sharks. The rewards are great, but so are the penalties. In my experience, there are so many other things to handle in running your business than using up energy on Debbie Downer and

Problem Pete. This energy should be going towards expanding the company. It just isn't worth it.

Each of you has to decide for yourselves. Welcome to the Big Leagues.

My Philosophy:

> **If someone creates problems and holds down their statistics, they make the game no fun.**
>
> **They need to go.**

***

"Peace is not absence of conflict, it is the ability to handle conflict by peaceful means."

Ronald Reagan, Former President of the U.S.

"There are some people who always seem angry and continuously look for conflict. Walk away from these people. The battle they're fighting isn't with you, it's with themselves."

Rashida Rowe, author

"You've got to know when to hold 'em, know when to fold 'em, know when to walk away, know when to run."

Kenny Rogers, entertainer and songwriter

***

I could give countless other examples of how I've noticed this phenomenon in my life, but I just want to share one more story with you that's slightly different. It is still just as telling and impactful as the last.

I had been in practice for ten years and the practice grew each year, sometimes faster than other times, but always growing.

I became very active in the community. I was United Way* President one year and Drive Chairman another year. I was president of my local church's administrative board and director of the youth group. We were very well ingrained* in the community.

However, in the third quarter of 1991, the grocery store that had anchored our strip mall for decades moved to a new facility across the street. I wasn't too concerned, at first. After all, I was very active in the community, and had been in practice for ten years. It might make a difference, but I had no worries.

How naïve of me.

Within six months all the other businesses moved out or went under. I was now in a dead strip mall with my office at the south end (fairly hidden from any main drive), then one hundred thousand empty square feet, with the

*United Way: a nonprofit organization that identifies and resolves pressing community issues through partnerships with schools, government agencies, businesses, organized labor, financial institutions, community development corporations, voluntary and neighborhood associations, the faith community, and others.

*Ingrained: deeply embedded and thus difficult to remove

If someone creates problems and holds down their statistics, they make the game no fun.

They need to go.

laundromat at the north end. I had twelve years left on a lease with no exit clause.

My revenue crashed during the next six months. We were down by 25%. I started operating under my breakeven point of paying the bills, started to run up balances on the credit cards, and my line of credit was all of a sudden maxed out.

I, quite honestly, couldn't believe it. The patients liked our practice and I'm definitely a good dentist. I had no idea that this turn of events would have such a dramatic impact on the practice.

Now the stakes were higher than when I first opened my practice. I had a much bigger house than my first one. I also had three kids, one of them a newborn; and I'm once again facing the situation of maybe having to lay off half the staff and possibly go to work part-time for someone else. My wife and I discussed it, but there was no way she could go back to work. Her salary would barely cover the childcare.

Out of sheer desperation, I became a client at a dental management company in Chicago that taught me the business basics of marketing, selling, and management. I took my staff to a couple of seminars and, all of a sudden, things started to get better. Within two months we had recovered back to the point where we were when the grocery store left.

However, I became very annoyed because, as things were turning around, there was dissent among the staff with some of the changes I made. Covert Connie was on the loose (I never employed anyone named Connie either).

I started to notice her having quiet conversations with other staff in her treatment room and the staff lounge that would end when I walked by. She copied articles on how bad things could get and distributed them amongst the staff. Once again, my stomach started to hurt.

So, I called her into my office and asked her what was going on. She went on and on about the changes I had made and how she feared that the practice was going to go down the drain. I took her into the staff lounge and showed her the statistic graphs that we kept on the wall. For six months straight, the statistics had been crashing and were now climbing at a good rate. Yet, she had never approached me with any concern until things had totally turned around and were going back into a viable range.

Where was she when the practice really *was* going down the drain? Why all of this concern when things are going dramatically better? She assured me that she was just trying to help.

My stomach continued to hurt.

This was not my first rodeo. I had seen this play before. So, I dismissed her, and guess what happened? With temporary replacements, we immediately did 25% over our best month in history.

My stomach felt much better.

I'm sure this isn't the first time you've heard the concept, "if you aren't part of the solution, you're part of the problem," or "the train is leaving the station, so you'd better get on board."

Well, I just want to go over with you my formula for handling problems and how this all applies. When the going gets tough, I have to take a look at all of my options. I get advice from people I know and trust. I keep all the Debbie Downers and Problem Petes away from me, and instead, go to Golden Gilda and Solution Sam.

I then weigh all the data and confront the worst-case scenario. How do I survive if it all goes wrong? How do I take care of my family if my planned solution doesn't work out?

First of all, I'm not going to die. I have the ability to produce. I mentioned earlier that I know a quadriplegic who is getting along just fine. He's an inspiration to me, and a personification*of what I'm trying to describe.

After figuring out how to handle the worst-case scenario, I use the data I gathered from those who believe in me and come up with a game plan. I solicit help from those people I trust, then we all go into action and handle the hell out of it. I'm always prepared for the current strategy to fail. It's not that I want or expect it to, but I already have an action plan of what I'm going to do if that happens. And I work my guts out, so I never have to resort to that.

The key is that, during this period, I'm ruthless about keeping everyone away from me who is not part of the

---

*Personification: representation of a thing or abstract thought as a person or by the human form

solution. If they don't believe in me, I have no use for them.

I'm fine if people bring up possible problems that can arise, and I have no use for a Yes Man who is simply propitiating* me to not get fired or to get a raise. But if you are going to bring up a problem, then you had better follow that up with an idea of how to handle it.

Basically, I expect the help of others to be genuine help. Not just spreading bad news in the name of help.

My advice is also to stop watching the news. Stop reading all kinds of negative crap online. Stop listening to naysayers blabbing on the social media platforms. These types love being a problem, and you can tell who is one of them pretty easily. There's no solution and it's all hopeless and bad.

I have my TV for sports, movies, and *Shark Tank*. That's about it. Maybe a *Big Bang Theory* episode every once in a while. The rest of the negative crap I have no use for.

Here's a simple way of looking at this whole situation. There is a concept called the Pareto Principle. It's also known as the 80/20 rule. It basically states that for many events, roughly 80% of the effects come from 20% of the causes. What that means is that, 80% of your problems are caused by 20% of the customers/staff/population. Many authors have referred to this.

---

*Propitiating: win or regain the favor of (a god, spirit, or person) by doing something only to please them

In my business experience, I've noticed that it works out this way to within almost a tenth of a percent. If I got in ten new patients, then two were nothing but a problem.

Of clients that I have sold other services to, 20% wouldn't comply; or what usually worked for everyone else, never worked for them.

Those that specialize in creating problems can often make a lot of noise; so much so, that all of a sudden, it seems like you no longer have *any* happy customers. When this happens, it's normal to start to wonder if you really know what you're doing, or maybe that what has always worked doesn't work anymore. Self-doubt, stress, and worry often start to creep in.

I once had a patient that made so much trouble when he came in that literally no one on the staff wanted him to come back. His wife, kids, and other relatives in the practice were great, but he was a royal pain. Fortunately for us, he wasn't a regular patient and only came in when there was a problem or when his wife was prodding him.

One day he came in to get his teeth cleaned and he started to make noise about something. I was done. I went back to my office and wrote down on a sheet of paper the names of his relatives that could leave the practice if I asked him to never return. It was about twelve patients that I could lose if they got upset about it.

I took a deep breath and made my decision. I went into the treatment room, sat in front of him, and said something to the effect that I thought it would be best if he found another dentist. I would be happy to forward his records wherever he wished, and that there was no charge for his cleaning and x-rays that day.

Everyone in the practice felt a huge relief. By the way, we didn't lose any of the other family members as patients. I evidently wasn't the only one that recognized he was a jerk and liked making trouble.

I once had a client write me a check for $74,000. For the next two days, he acted like he owned us. His attitude completely changed, and he became belligerent and noncompliant. We had a staff meeting and decided that we didn't want a long-term relationship with him no matter how much he paid. There was a bit of paperwork that went back and forth, but two days later, I put the check into a FedEx envelope and sent it back to him. No amount of money is worth having to put up with that much trouble.

Of course, give it your best shot to sort it all out. However, if it doesn't, there is really only one course of action. Get them out of your world.

My Philosophy:

If you're going to be a problem, you can't be in my game.

The solution is to push forward with what has always worked. Try to handle the noise with good communication. Be willing to refund a client/customer or dismiss a staff member. Then move on and get back to what has usually worked in the past.

This is a definite tightwire walk across the Falls. If you don't use good communication to try to handle something and just dismiss everyone around you, then you'll be left alone. However, if you just let all the noise continue, then you'll end up stressed out and sometimes sick.

Again, there might have been times when I have dismissed someone that didn't need to be dismissed. I apologize to all of them for my errors. At the time, it seemed for the best.

We have all had our down moments when we weren't really helping a situation. We have all had momentary lapses in our optimistic point of view. This is not an absolute, and no one is perfect, but the difference is that a momentary lapse is different from a normal operating basis.

What I've found is that, once I sit down with Golden Gilda and Solution Sam, I snap out of it. Trusted friends and advisors are priceless!

The tightwire walk across Niagara Falls will have many moments where you almost go over the edge. You have to be tough to survive. It takes courage to confront and handle the day-to-day operations of business.

Persist and eliminate anyone from your game that makes it no fun.

If you would like help in applying the concepts that I am writing about, you can get a free PDF of exercises I have created to help you get more out of reading "FUN AT WORK."

Simply go to www.funatworkthebook.com for the download.

Fun at Work

13

There Is No Future Without Vision

Every business starts with an idea. Watch *Shark Tank*, every budding* entrepreneur that has the courage to walk into the tank started with an idea. They thought they could do something better than another person who was already doing it; or they had a brand-new idea to fill a need that no one else could.

My mom makes these amazing homemade granola bars. The kids always say, "Grandma, these are awesome! You should go into business making granola bars!"

And that's how a business gets started, or not.

After there's an idea, someone has to come up with a plan that enables work to get done, and an ability to make it happen. If the plan sounds doable, and the person with the idea really wants it badly enough, then action occurs. If the plan is correct, and managed properly, the idea is created in the physical universe by those who do the labor.

Basically put, ideas lead to a plan. Managers get employees to execute the plan and create the product or provide the service. If the product or service is desired by the people, they pay money for it and the company then makes money in order to continue doing it.

Let's take two fictitious guys from Michigan, Tom and Joe, so that we can get an idea of how a new business could go.

***Budding:** beginning and showing signs of promise in a particular career or field

201

Fun at Work

Tom lives in Traverse City and Joe lives in Lansing. They each really enjoy yard work and landscaping. With every spare minute they have, they are outside puttering in the yard, planting flowers and shrubs. They help their neighbors and relatives for free because it's fun, and they're each kind of tired of their boring 9-5 jobs. Each of them has the same idea: "I'm going to go into business for myself and mow lawns and do landscaping. I think I can make a living at this."

Tom knows some people that he has helped before that have said they would hire him if he ever decided to go into business, so he launches his endeavor in April by putting his riding mower on a trailer and using his truck to go from job to job. He's very excited that, by June, he is making enough money to pay his bills. His wife is very impressed.

He has a Facebook page, and his customers are happy. Pretty soon he's putting in twelve-hour days. He comes home at night exhausted, takes his shower and usually falls asleep on the couch after a few bites of dinner.

His wife wants to take the family on their summer vacation but he's way too busy for that. Grass grows, and his customers would be upset if he missed a week. It could cost him business and he's worked too hard to build it up. His wife is now upset.

He has the idea of hiring someone to help him, but that would cost him money, so he prefers to just work harder. Soon, he is turning away business because there are only so many hours in a week; besides, he's getting tired.

The fall comes, and the grass growth slows down. In preparation for winter, he stays busy raking leaves. By Thanksgiving, the leaves are all raked and there's not much to do. He works each day repairing his equipment and resting up from the exhausting summer.

By January, the extra money that he made is now gone because he has no income and he starts delivering pizza. His wife now has to get a second job and she's really pissed!

Luckily, April came along because things were really getting ugly at home. By June he's working sixty to eighty hours a week. He is putting as much money in the bank as he can, so the next winter isn't as bad as the last.

Five years later, they still haven't had a vacation.

Now let's take Joe. Joe knows some people that he's helped before that have said they would hire him if he ever decided to go into business. He launches his endeavor in April by putting his riding mower on a trailer and using his truck to go from job to job. He's very excited that, by June, he is making enough money to pay his bills. His wife is very impressed.

Very soon he is putting in twelve-hour days, comes home at night exhausted, takes his shower and usually falls asleep on the couch after a few bites of dinner.

He realizes that he's making money but working much harder than he ever has in his life. He's now turning away jobs because he doesn't have enough hours in the day. Luckily, his neighbor's son Jason is home from college, so

Joe hires him to cut grass. Joe just has to do the landscaping now.

It costs him money to pay Jason, but the landscaping is more profitable, so it's more than worth it to him. Jason nets* him an extra $200 per week. He believes that it's better than turning away business.

Joe lands a big landscaping job. He gets Jason to round up some of his college friends to put in a few extra hours to finish the job in a week. The customer is extremely happy because the other companies were too busy and couldn't get to it for three weeks. After all, it's July, and everyone is very busy.

By the end of the summer, Joe has three employees mowing grass. Jason goes back to school, but he and his crew stay busy raking leaves and helping people get their property ready for winter.

The first snow hits after Thanksgiving, and Joe puts a blade on his truck to remove snow from driveways. He rents a truck to keep his other staff busy on driveways and sidewalks.

By April, twelve months later, he has made double what he did when he was working for someone else. Over the winter, he has lined up enough yard and landscaping work to need to hire six more staff.

Jason graduated from college and was having a hard time finding a job, so Joe hired him to manage all the crews.

*Nets: produced by way of profit; YIELD

In conclusion, Tom was self-employed, but Joe became a CEO.

Actually, Tom's business owned *him*. He did all the work.

Joe owned and expanded his business by doing less and less physical labor. He created a vision for the company, sold a manager on the vision, and hired others to do the work.

Based on this, here's the formula that I have used to really win:

1. Have a clear Basic Purpose for the business. Something that helps a lot of people. Something that excites me and gets me out of bed when the going gets tough.
2. Hire, or create, a Manager to run the day-to-day activities. They *must* be sold on my vision and Basic Purpose. That will get them out of bed in the morning when the going gets tough. I'm more interested in managers that are motivated by my purpose than motivated by money. I will make sure they are well-paid when we are making money, but if they aren't excited about the purpose, they will leave for a dollar an hour raise from someone else.
3. Cooperative workers that like the product or service and agree with my vision, are critical. They are easier to manage and work harder.
4. Uncooperative managers and workers are replaced. In my experience, about 80% are willing.
5. Have fun.

Now, I have a real team with everyone pulling in the same direction. And we all need each other.

Tom was Self-Employed.

Joe became a CEO.

It's totally like a football team. All eleven players are needed on offense and all eleven players are needed on defense. There are certain positions that require more skill, but every position is important. Make last year's Super Bowl champ play this season with only ten players and they won't win any games.

My Philosophy:

If I'm going to be a CEO, it's my responsibility to create a Basic Purpose and vision that excites people, and constantly expands the company.

***

"The secret to successful hiring is this: look for the people who want to change the world."

Marc Benioff, Salesforce CEO

***

What does the CEO do? They make sure that the company's Basic Purpose is maintained, and they always create strategic plans for the expansion of the company. They are always looking for great managers and cooperative workers. Junior Managers become Senior Managers. The most cooperative and motivated workers become Junior Managers.

If the employees watch those who take responsibility get promoted and make more money, then they will be motivated to move up. They won't leave if someone offers them a dollar an hour more because they see a future staying where they're at.

If I'm going to be a CEO,
it's my responsibility to create a
Basic Purpose and vision
that excites people;
and constantly expands the
company.

It's the job of the CEO to keep everyone interested in the vision and use the managers to help create effective Strategic Game Plans. The CEO manages the Managers, and the Managers manage the employees.

And everyone is important. A CEO can have great ideas, but he is nothing without managers and workers. Good managers and workers are always looking for a great boss with vision, a good purpose, and someone who is fair. Cooperative workers are always grateful for a passionate manager that cares about them and the purpose of the company.

This is a winning combination that creates a dynasty. It can last for decades, or longer.

I'll add this. As the CEO or Manager, you had better use the people around you. Give them more responsibility. Train them. Keep them engaged in the game. If you don't, then the best ones will leave for greener pastures. If you do, you will create a dedicated team that will walk across hot coals for you.

To pull this off, you will need two critical elements. Good training materials, and patience.

Good training materials are a form of communication. I could write an entire book on just this; but let me cover a few basics.

All the technical terms of the position and industry must be defined and written down. I promise that, if they don't understand a term, there will be a mistake and possible disaster just around the corner. There should be training manuals with pictures, and possibly videos, that clearly describe all the components of the job. Have them study these materials, quiz or drill them, and demonstrate to them how to do the job. Then make them demonstrate to you that they can.

Show them how to do the simplest of tasks. Watch them do it. Then leave them alone and see what happens. Check up on them every thirty minutes or so to see how they're doing. If they have made a mistake, then correct them and make sure they understand the terms. Then, let them go at it again.

Patience is the key. You can't expect them to do the job as well as you can. They will make mistakes. Some of those mistakes might cost you some money, but if you aren't patient enough to get someone trained to take over for you, then you will never work yourself out of the job. You will be overworked and not have a vacation for five years.

The better the training materials, and the better your patience, the greater the chance of ending up with a cooperative employee or manager.

My Philosophy:

It's my responsibility to make sure the training materials can easily get a new person started on the job.

However, here comes that damned tightwire walk again.

If you hang onto a trainee for too long, then it slows down your expansion and costs you even more money. They chew up a lot of time and make so many mistakes that they aren't worth the effort. Then they have to be dismissed and you have to start over.

We have all made the mistake of waiting too long to fire an employee. If someone has been with you for a while, I can understand and sympathize with you. I think it's the worst part of owning your own business. I hate firing people, but sometimes it needs to be done.

Let's take a look at the new person. They need to be showing daily progress on the simple tasks they are being given. If you give them something simple to do and they mess up, then you show them again, but if you leave and thirty minutes later it's messed up again, how does this have a happy ending two weeks, or two months, or two years from now?

If you dismiss them today, you probably still have another one or two that you liked during the interview process. Call them up and get them to come in.

As a matter of fact, if you want to end up with one good employee you should probably hire three. You will probably protest and say that you can't afford them, but here's how it will probably go down: You hire three and, on the first day only two show up. You start training those two, and within a week or two, one of them quits or you dismiss them. Now, you have the one you wanted from the beginning. You just saved yourself all that time by bringing them all in at once rather than one at a time.

Generally speaking, I want any employee to be able to do a moderately good job within the first two weeks. I need to be able to trust that I can give them a task and have them not mess it up while getting it done in a reasonable amount of time. If they make too many mistakes, or are too slow, then I need to move on. Here's where I can't be too patient. That slows us all down because other good staff are covering for the new guy.

If your training materials are good, this won't be that big a deal. Have new hires watch videos and look at the pictures of the job while you are working, then you show them what to do. Leave them alone and see what happens.

You will eventually find a superstar. You leave them alone for thirty minutes, and they are already onto the second or third thing. Those will be your managers of the future. Give them lots of responsibility, fast, and they will blossom.

I don't want to give the wrong impression and lead you to believe that everyone needs to be a superstar. Cooperative employees who are loyal, show up on time, and give you a good day's work with rare mistakes, are priceless. Many of them don't want to move up into Management or take on more responsibilities. I love 'em! They fit in perfectly to what I'm trying to accomplish and stay stably for a long time.

***

"Always treat your employees exactly as you want them to treat your best customers."

Stephen R. Covey, Author

***

Finally, I think work should be enjoyable. It is the CEO's responsibility to create a pleasant work environment. I know of a CEO that has a Pilates instructor in three times a week. Another has an entire area for video game competitions amongst the staff.

The point is, a pleasant work environment combined with a focused dedication to fulfill the Basic Purpose of the company will make you a great CEO with a large organization.

Now how do you make it last?

If you would like help in applying the concepts that I am writing about, you can get a free PDF of exercises I have created to help you get more out of reading "FUN AT WORK."

Simply go to www.funatworkthebook.com for the download.

Fun at Work

14

Creating a Dynasty That Lasts for Decades or More

***

"No more romanticizing about how cool it is to be an entrepreneur. It's a struggle to save your company's life – and your own skin – every day of the week."

Spencer Fry, co-founder of CarbonMade

***

Every community has a few businesses that have been around for decades. They have naturally done a lot of what I've written about. They take great care of their customers and staff, provide a needed quality product or service, and treat people the way they want to be treated. The owners are usually tough, smart, very hard workers.

These businesses are usually family-owned and are passed on from one generation to the next. You can imagine how this happens. As the kids are growing up, they go into the business with their parents, they play there, and then start doing small jobs, i.e. shredding, filing, cleaning up, etc.

Of course, there are business conversations around the dinner table; and as the kids get older, they are given more responsibilities. In their teens, they are put in charge of different projects or areas. Then one day, Mom and Dad go on vacation and the kids run the show. They make a few mistakes, but because they are family, their errors are tolerated and corrected. A decade or two later, mom and dad retire and spend six months of the year in Florida.

We have also all seen the successful family business that was sold to someone else and it eventually went under. The new owners thought they had a better idea. They came in and changed everything that had been working for years, or decades. They violated all the successful actions of those who started the business.

In my experience, it's usually because the new owners were chasing profits, whereas the one who established the successful company was all about the passion of helping others.

My dad and uncle owned a restaurant in a small farm town of three-thousand people in Indiana. It was very successful and put my brother, me, and my cousins through college; but they sold it to someone who wouldn't listen and changed everything about it. This person was able to hang on by his fingernails for a few years, but eventually went bankrupt. How sad. A thriving family business destroyed in a short period of time.

There's no reason that you can't follow a successful pattern that will have your business around for decades or even centuries—with or without kids to turn the business over to. Let's pull together all of the concepts of this book. This is the recipe. If you don't leave out any ingredients, you will generally succeed.

Find something you are passionate about that helps others survive better; basically, make their life better with something they need or want. Decide to start a business providing that product or service. Write down a clearly stated Basic Purpose for doing it.

Create your Strategic Game Plan. This is your starting point. It gets the ball rolling. I can almost guarantee that you will have to change it, but it's a place to start.

This is where your Action Plan comes into play. Using your available resources, figure out the logistics of what to do first, second, and third. Then START! Don't sit around planning, and planning, and planning. START!

You will have to figure it out and make adjustments on the run.

You are producing something now. This is the hard work of making mistakes and correcting them by finding out what you can improve to better help the consumer. Just be careful to never lose sight of why you are doing it and what you want out of it for yourself, your family, your employees, and your customers.

Always be expanding your vision and sharing it with the entire team.

Always have Profit as the end result of your Strategic Game Plan and your Action Plan. Otherwise, you will never be around for very long or be killing yourself to scrape out a living.

Always try to deliver more than promised or advertised. Put the customer first.

That being said, you MUST learn how to balance customer service with profits. Walk the tightwire.

Here is where you must always be looking for your replacement. Look for someone who is passionate about the company, someone you can apprentice for a few years, someone to gradually give more and more responsibility to and someone you can be patient with. Like one of your kids.

Always be looking for good managers and cooperative, productive workers. Notice how you are treated when you are the customer. I have no problem hiring someone away from another business if they have treated me awesomely.

Keep anyone who creates problems away from you. It doesn't matter how much that customer is willing to pay you; or how critical you think that one employee is to your business. Dump the negative out of your life. It will all of a sudden become much easier and a lot more fun.

Stay in communication with those around you and let them know what's happening. Let them know what the score of the game is, but never alarm them with bad news or anything that might cause them to lose confidence in the company. Once the storm has passed, and you've handled it, you can give them the good news that a disaster was averted; don't scare them while in the middle of it.

If your business is already up and running, simply look back over this recipe and put in the ingredients that you skipped over or didn't do well enough. It's never too late to start over or recreate your business.

The CEO has to be able to be in a helicopter and look down on all aspects of the company and see the big picture. They have to take responsibility for everything that goes on in the company—good and bad. The buck stops at the top.

The key is for the CEO to promote a sense of ownership and pride amongst everyone in the company. There really are people out there who will care as much for the company as you do, but that team has to be created. It seldom happens by accident. The best thing to do is to create an environment where people are rewarded for the successes of the company and the real players will rise to the top. They will step forward and make their areas really produce. Then you promote them and pay them more—mainly with nice production and profitability bonuses.

***

"I'm convinced that about half of what separates the successful entrepreneurs from the non-successful ones is pure perseverance."

Steve Jobs, Co-Founder and CEO, Apple

"Never, never, never give up."

Winston Churchill, British Prime Minister

"Make your team feel respected, empowered and genuinely excited about the company's mission."

Tim Westergren, Pandora Founder

***

We sometimes resist problems in the company. There are areas that we know are out of control. We don't inspect them because we aren't really sure what to do or maybe don't even like that particular function or area of the company.

I promise you that area of the company will one day flare up and be a problem if it isn't addressed now. So, if you don't want to work in that area, put someone in charge of it and let them fix it. Give them responsibility for the area and let them get on with it.

In business, there will typically be one or more major situations that will arise each year. Something unexpected is always just around the corner. My advice is to use that situation to grow.

When the going gets tough, I rally the trusted people around me. I ask them for their help. Good staff love to help. They will stand by you and help you through the toughest times. If there's someone you thought you could count on during a crisis who abandons you to clock out at 5:00, then they just showed you what is most important to them; something other than helping you solve the problems.

Those who help you through these moments of stress are priceless. They should be rewarded with some sort of bonus, i.e. a night out to a great restaurant for them and their spouse, a day or two off, a three-day cruise, etc. The key is to let them know that you really appreciated their support.

Use the problems that arise to find out just who the dedicated and the able are amongst your competent workers and managers. You probably know how to attack the problem, so go over it with them and turn them loose on it. It will probably take them longer to figure it out, and they might mess it up at first, but help them handle it. They will feel great about themselves and their job, and you now have an employee that's just a bit more capable than they were before.

That's how you work yourself out of a job.

I frequently hear that someone was all trained up and then left the company to start their own competing venture. That's usually created by the one doing the complaining. They didn't challenge that talented employee enough. They also probably didn't reward them for extra effort and they definitely didn't talk to them and find out how they were doing or what their goals were.

The focus was usually short-term income for the owner, versus long-term stability for the company.

The up-and-coming superstar was not rewarded with nice production bonuses or sold a small share of the company. That probably would have kept them around. Is the extra pay for you, by not giving it to them, really worth the agony and effort of finding the next superstar? I never thought it was.

In my story in the previous chapter about Joe the landscaper, he hired the college kid, Jason, from next door for the summer. Let's say Jason is a hard worker. He shows up on time and takes responsibility for his tasks. Joe should then just keep giving him more and more responsibility and reward his efforts.

Jason has one more year of college and doesn't know exactly what he wants to do yet. I would tell him to come back after graduation and I'll give him a job managing the crews. I would also be telling him about my plans to continue to expand into another market in a neighboring city or county. I'd let him know that, if he works hard, I'll make him a partner in that market.

Give great employees and managers a game. Keep giving them your jobs and responsibilities. Make them more important in the day-to-day operations, reward them, and get them to take ownership. Let them help you solve your problems. If you do that properly, I'd be surprised if they ever leave.

My Philosophy:

> **Good Executives set real goals and motivate the employees to play the game of reaching them.**

Don't have kids to take over the operation when you retire? Sure, you can sell to an entrepreneur, take the money and run; but, how will you feel if it all goes under in a few years? If your goal and Basic Purpose are right, you wouldn't be very happy or proud of that.

How about leaving a legacy? When I sold my practice in 1993, the staff and my associate had been trained on how to make it run because I had already turned over many of my key responsibilities. I'm proud to say that he paid off

Good Executives set real goals and motivate the employees to play the game of reaching them.

his ten-year loan in five years and recently moved into a new facility. That's exactly what I wanted for all of them and my patients.

Groom your successor. Then work until you're a hundred. By the time you've been in business for ten or twenty years, or more, your greatest value will be your experience and connections. Stay active in the business but turn over the day-to-day challenges to your replacement.

Become a consultant to your own company. There are so many ways to participate and contribute without working sixty-hour weeks; but you have to empower and reward those around you as you grow the company.

There are so many factors that have to be balanced, e.g. keeping the customers happy, pricing the product or service properly to be able to sell it for a profit, keeping the employees happy, paying taxes, having a life outside of the business, etc., etc., etc.

It's a tremendous accomplishment to be able to walk the tightwire of owning your own business. The rewards of the wins are balanced by the pressure, stress and constant threat of losses. Those who can't properly balance all the variables, or take the pressure, fall off.

The toughest owners learn from their mistakes and climb back up on the tightwire stronger and wiser. The less dedicated and motivated move on to other things.

My advice is to learn from my mistakes and apply what I've written in this book. I suggest you read it two or three times right now, and then review it once a year. Bad habits can easily sneak back into the game.

Have all of your partners, executives, and managers read it also. Then listen to their input and include them in key decisions. Give them problems to go figure out and to handle. It promotes taking an ownership role for the company and their future.

If you take full responsibility for the continuous expansion of your company, then it will always be there to provide for you. It's something that you will be able to control into the future and be so much more predictable than the gamble of relying on a retirement account and the possibility of running out of money if you live too long.

Besides, if you do this right, it's a lot more fun than golfing and fishing every day.

My Philosophy:

Apply what you have learned in this book, review it annually, and you will succeed.

If you would like help in applying the concepts that I am writing about, you can get a free PDF of exercises I have created to help you get more out of reading "FUN AT WORK."

Simply go to www.funatworkthebook.com for the download.

Apply what you have learned in this book, review it annually, and you will succeed.

Acknowledgements

I need to write these acknowledgements to those who have supported, encouraged, and helped me in all my endeavors; however, this carries risk along with it as I could forget to recognize someone who has contributed to my success. I'll apologize in advance as any omission will have been unintentional.

I need to start at the beginning. My mom and dad opened a restaurant in a small Indiana farm town of three-thousand with my dad's brother and wife the month after I was born. The restaurant business is known to be very hard work with incredibly slim margins of profit.

I learned about persistence and perseverance from them after our entire operation, and our home, was destroyed by a tornado when I was nine years old. I learned about hard work from the time I was four years old washing dishes on a flipped over milk crate because I was too short to reach the sink. I learned how to make a profit through conversations with my dad about how much to charge for a hot fudge sundae and a hamburger. I learned about customer service as I saw how they handled disgruntled patrons.

I thank them for my entrepreneurial spirit and the lessons that they passed on to me.

Then there is my awesome wife, Sandra. She is truly a saint. Not all of my business adventures have succeeded; and none were ever easy or without stress. She has *never* lost faith in me and has always been my number one supporter and cheerleader. I want her to know that I couldn't have done any of this without her.

Next there are my kids, Vince, Neil, and Abby. My endeavors have oftentimes meant that I missed birthday parties, soccer games, and bedtime stories. Not once have they ever given me a hard time about any of that. The other amazing thing is that none of them gave me any trouble when they were growing up. They never created any drama that pulled my attention onto some major problem. They now either work for me in my businesses or have their own business, and I am infinitely proud of each of them.

Each of them is married and I want to acknowledge their spouses, Michelle, Katlin, and Aaron. Each of them is as amazing as my kids. Again, they back me up in my endeavors and do everything to help me pull off my next crazy idea. I love each of you very much and thank you for your contributions to our family.

I want to acknowledge my brother, Jon. He also owns his own business and we have had many stimulating conversations over the years about being an entrepreneur and our various strategies. There was a time in my life when all of my friends abandoned me because some of the decisions I made were unreal to them. He *never* lost faith in me and I consider him one of my best friends.

I also want to thank Jon's wife, Cindy, and his daughters, Stefany, and Stacia. I truly admire how you all work together and how you have all supported me with your positive feedback and attitudes. And for *always* believing in me.

I also have amazing friends. Each of you has been a source of eternal encouragement and belief in what I have done and the games we have played together. You know who you are, and I consider your friendship priceless. By the way, I have a lot more in store for us.

It would be impossible to acknowledge those who have worked for and with me. This book is about you. I have learned something from each of you; all of you have also contributed in your own ways. Thank you.

I have quoted many successful leaders, authors, motivational speakers, and personalities in this work. Thanks for passing along your wisdom to me. Your words have meant so much to me. I hope to pass the ways that you have inspired me along to others in these pages.

And finally, I need to acknowledge PresenterMedia.com. They have a fantastic subscription service that I have used to bring my power point presentations to life. I love the creativity they bring to their game. They have so graciously allowed me to use their art for the illustrations in this book. I highly recommend their services for your presentations and videos.

I have surrounded myself with amazing and dedicated people that have helped me create an ideal life. I want that for everyone who reads this book...an ideal life. I've written it in such a way that I hope it's easy for you to duplicate and understand. I will be here to help you if you want me to.

We'd love to hear from you!

To contact Matterhorn Business Development and find out how Greg and his team can help you and your business, call us or email us:

727-810-3022
info@MatterhornBizDev.com
www.MatterhornBizDev.com

MATTERHORN
BUSINESS DEVELOPMENT
IF YOU KNOW US, YOU WIN.

About the Author

Greg Winteregg is an internationally recognized entrepreneur, lecturer and management consultant that specializes in teaching small business owners how to reach the maximum potential for their business.

He's lectured to and worked with tens of thousands of business owners in ten countries across three continents and built several successful small businesses himself.

By 38, he'd built his first business up to the point where he was semi-retired prior to selling it and becoming a partner in what has since became one of the largest consulting firms of its kind in North America. He currently owns or is a partner in three companies, lives in the Tampa Bay Area and has been happily married to his college sweetheart, Sandra for 38 years. Together they are the proud parents and grandparents of three children and three grandchildren.

www.ingramcontent.com/pod-product-compliance
Lightning Source LLC
Chambersburg PA
CBHW040917210326
41597CB00030B/5104